IESE CITIES IN MOTION:
INTERNATIONAL URBAN BEST PRACTICES

CITIES AND THE ECONOMY:
FUELING GROWTH, JOBS AND INNOVATION

VOLUME 3

PROF. PASCUAL BERRONE
PROF. JOAN ENRIC RICART COSTA
ANA ISABEL DUCH T-FIGUERAS

Copyright © 2016 Pascual Berrone, Joan Enric Ricart Costa, Ana Isabel Duch T-Figueras

All rights reserved.

ISBN-13: 978-1535320818

ISBN-10: 1535320818

Preface to the Book Series

"IESE CITIES IN MOTION:
International Urban Best Practices"

The world is experiencing the largest increase in urban growth in history. Today, more than half of the world's population lives in cities and it is forecast that the percentage of urban residents in the global population will increase to almost 70% by 2050. This unprecedented growth in urbanization has the potential to bring significant benefits for citizens, such as new jobs and well-being, along with overall economic growth. However, rapid urbanization also multiplies the number, size and complexity of the challenges faced by cities, such as increasing pressure on scarce resources, greater demand for basic infrastructure and public services, as well as greater socioeconomic inequality.

Cities must be able to solve economic, social and environmental problems simultaneously, in all cases with the aim of improving the welfare and quality of life of their residents. In their search for sustainable, equitable, connected and innovative city models, municipal leaders around the world look at the experiences of other cities to get ideas and study best practices. Although there is no "one size fits all" solution, this book series aims to help city managers in their endeavors to create urban areas that are environmentally, economically and socially sustainable. With this objective, this series will examine some of the actions, projects and initiatives that have had the best results in cities internationally, so that other cities around the world can build on the most successful approaches and adapt them to their local realities and needs.

The book series is structured based on the IESE Cities in Motion model, which includes an innovative approach to the governance of cities and a new urban model for the 21st century based on 10 key areas or dimensions: human capital, social cohesion, the economy, public management, governance, mobility and transportation, the environment, urban planning, technology and international outreach. Each volume in this series provides an overview of the main challenges regarding a specific dimension and exhibits some of the most successful initiatives and actions that have been adopted regarding that area in different cities around the world. Despite the fact that each area is covered in a separate volume of its own, all the key areas must be seen as different parts of a system that works as one. All the dimensions are interconnected and actions in one area affect other areas at the same time. Therefore, the available resources must be shared and managed together in order to achieve sustainable, lively, healthy and safe cities.

With this book series, we aim to contribute to the debate on smart urban governance by developing valuable ideas and innovative tools that can lead to smarter and more sustainable cities, while promoting real change at the local level and improving people's quality of life. We believe that current urban challenges are not only problems to be solved, but also opportunities to be exploited.

Prior volumes of this series:

Vol. 1: *Cities and the Environment: The Challenge of Becoming Green and Sustainable,* CreateSpace, 2016.

See, "Greening Up in the City". Available at: http://www.amazon.com/dp/1523965789.

"Responsible for the vast majority of the world's energy use and greenhouse gas emissions, urban areas are also the main contributors to air, noise, water and land pollution. Moreover, cities generate large quantities of waste, are voracious consumers of natural resources, and they are particularly vulnerable to natural disasters and climate change. Given the current rates of urbanization, the environmental impacts of cities are of urgent concern. This first volume of the series focuses on the effects of urbanization on our planet, analyzing the main environmental challenges that city governments face, and offering a catalog of international urban best practices on environmental issues."

Vol. 2: *Cities and Mobility & Transportation: Towards the Next Generation of Urban Mobility,* CreateSpace, 2016.

See, "Setting the Wheels in Motion for Sustainable Transportation". Available at: https://www.amazon.com/dp/1533358141.

"As cities grow, the demand for mobility escalates. This stresses existing urban transport systems and infrastructures, exacerbates widespread traffic, and increases road accidents and fatalities. It also increases greenhouse gas emissions and air and noise pollution, causing serious health concerns and grave environmental repercussions. Thus, ensuring a sustainable and efficient distribution of people, goods and services is essential to cities' social and economic development. This second volume of the series focuses on the main urban mobility and transportation trends and challenges, and compiles a catalog of international best practices on sustainable urban mobility."

Contents

Preface iii
1. Introduction 1
2. Urban Economic Trends and Challenges 5
   2.1 Accelerated Economic Growth 5
      Sectors of the Urban Economy 9
      Household Incomes and Emerging Economies 11
      Rising Inequalities 14
      Informal Economy 15
   2.2 Employment Generation 16
      Unemployment 17
      Informal Employment 18
   2.3 Economic Agglomeration and Urban Productivity 20
      Competitiveness 22
   2.4 A Connected World: Cities as Hubs of the Global Economy 23
3. Cities as Enablers of Sustainable Economic Prosperity:
   Smart Solutions and Best Practices 27
   3.1 Infrastructure and Urban Services 31
   3.2 A Good Business Environment for Competitiveness 34
      3.2.1 Ease of Doing Business 34
      3.2.2 Entrepreneurship 37
         SMEs 40
      3.2.3 Innovation 43
         Innovation Districts 44
         Incubators and Accelerators 48
      3.2.4 Economic Clusters 51
         Special Economic Zones (SEZ) 59

3.3 Facilitating the Transformation into New Urban Economies 61

    3.3.1 Digital Economy and the Economy of Data 61

        Big Data 63

        Open Data 65

        Internet-of-Things 69

    3.3.2 The Green and the Circular Economy 70

        Green Economy 71

        Circular Economy 72

    3.3.3 The Sharing Economy 75

    3.3.4 The Creative Economy 80

4. Concluding Remarks 85

5. References 89

6. Appendix I: Additional Resources 97

7. Appendix II: Cities in Motion Index – Economic Dimension 99

1. Introduction

The ability of cities to generate income, employment and well-being for its inhabitants is one of the main drivers behind today's high urbanization rates. Cities concentrate large amounts of people, firms and economic activities, as well as public services and infrastructures. This abundant concentration of resources and public intervention allows for important economic advantages and externalities, such as strategic location, proximity, big local market demand, human resources and diversity. Consequently, **cities are becoming indispensable engines for the economic development of regions and nations around the world**.

Today, urban areas generate around 80% of worldwide Gross Domestic Product (GDP), and their contribution to the global economy is only expected to keep on rising. Additionally, this economic growth and economic development in cities allow them to become important enablers of value creation and employment facilitation. Cities attract people with diverse origins, customs, traditions and cultures looking for prospects of a better life. As a result, cities are not only places where workers find employment opportunities, they also create more diverse social communities, creating a positive environment for new ideas to emerge, fostering creativity, dynamism, innovation and knowledge diffusion.

Although cities provide important economic opportunities for individuals and firms around the world, the concentration of highly productive activities in urban areas does not spontaneously result in a better quality of life and well-being for all citizens. Agglomeration in cities also has the potential to yield perilous challenges and can result in negative externalities, such as higher inequalities, unemployment, poverty, increased social segregation and social tensions, higher crime rates, shortages of physical and social infrastructure, rising costs of urban infrastructure, traffic congestion, pollution, a huge strain on the world's natural resources and the environment, price increases and a lack of affordable housing.[1]

A major challenge for city leaders is to reinforce the role of their cities as drivers of economic growth and employment creation, while solving the abovementioned challenges. The way city managers allocate resources, promote innovation and create employment affect how economies grow. To bring the benefits of urban economic development and reduce the risks and associated problems, city managers need to plan for sustainable futures through a strategic "sustainable smart growth" approach. This means **balancing economic development, social progress and environmental issues in the most ecological and equitable way possible**.

If local leaders choose the right policies when promoting economic growth, supported by enforceable legal frameworks, they can create new businesses and jobs; optimize resources; and offer enormous potential for wealth creation and better living standards at different levels of society and government. City managers must leverage their position and work together with the private sector, citizens, academia and NGOs to lead urban transformations that can achieve prosperity and well-being for people and businesses alike, while ensuring sustainability and equity.

---

[1] Some of these issues will be examined in this volume, while others will be examined in other volumes of this series. For instance, challenges related to pollution and energy consumption are covered in the first volume of the series, *Cities and The Environment* (Berrone, Ricart, and Duch T-Figueras, 2016b); challenges related to traffic congestion are examined in the second volume, *Cities and Mobility and Transportation* (Berrone, Ricart, and Duch T-Figueras, 2016a); and the challenges related to inequality, poverty and social tensions will be analyzed in the book *Cities and Social Cohesion*.

This book reviews the trends and challenges of economic development in urban areas and debates what city governments can do to foster sustainable urban economic development. Following this introduction, Section 2 discusses various trends and prospects, as well as frames the challenges of economic development in cities. Section 3 highlights international urban best practices fostering economic development and discusses a few notable successful initiatives. The last section of the book offers some concluding remarks.

***

2. Urban Economic Trends and Challenges

Urban areas are the main driving force behind national economies. They are centers of economic activities, business opportunities, social services, education, healthcare, technological innovation, culture and leisure. As a result, cities create both employment and well-being. However, they can also be places where some of the most important challenges of the 21st century, such as inequality, unemployment, segregation and poverty, are concentrated and exacerbated. This section outlines some of the main economic development trends and challenges that cities around the world are currently facing, or are likely to face in the upcoming decades.

2.1 Accelerated Economic Growth

As mentioned in the introduction, **cities generate around 80% of global GDP** and over 60% of national GDP in many countries. Of the largest 750 cities in the world, three-quarters have grown faster than their national economies since the early 2000s (Kilroy, Francis, Mukim, and Negri, 2015). In fact, the prosperity and economic growth of regions and nations around the world is increasingly dependent on the economic performance of their cities (UN-Habitat, 2016).

Urban-based economic activities account for up to 55% of gross national product (GNP) in low-income countries, 73% in middle-income countries and 85% in high-income countries (United Nations, 2014). This means that in almost every country in the world, urban areas generate more than half of their respective nation's prosperity. What is more, cities' contribution to national income is often substantially greater than the percentage of the nation's population they represent (Figure 1). For instance, Paris accounts for the 16% of the population of France, but generates 27% of the country's GDP; Kinshasa hosts some 13% of the population of the Democratic Republic of the Congo but accounts for 85% of the city's GDP; and 12% of the population of the Philippines live in metro Manila, while the city contributes 47% of the GDP (UN-Habitat, 2016).

Figure 1: Urban share of national income vs. urban share of national population

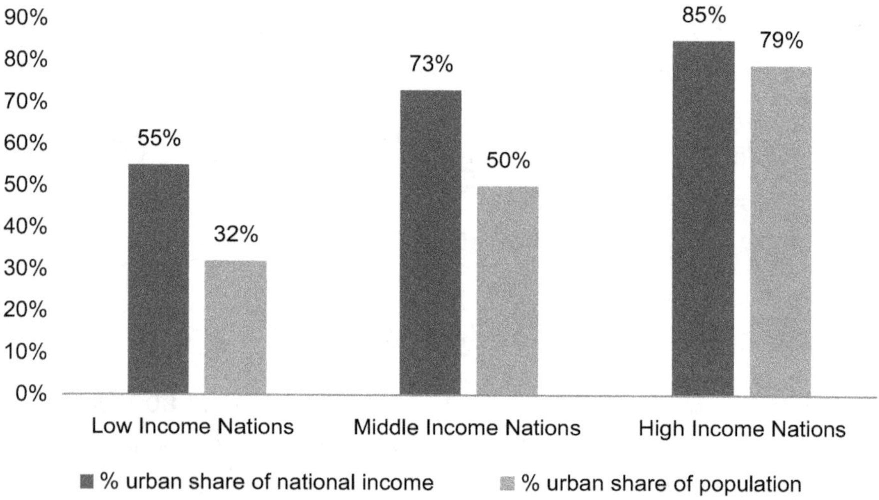

Nation Category	% urban share of national income	% urban share of population
Low Income Nations	55%	32%
Middle Income Nations	73%	50%
High Income Nations	85%	79%

Source: Weiss (2006) based on the World Bank Development Indicators.

Not only are urban areas unquestionable engines driving national and global economic growth, this economic growth is also concentrated in a reduced number of major urban centers and metropolitan areas. Today, **some 600 cities form the backbone of the global economy** (The Economist, 2014). According to McKinsey Global Institute (MGI), the top 100 cities in the world were responsible for the 38% of the total GDP in 2007 (or around US$21

Chapter 2: Urban Economic Trends and Challenges

trillion)[2] (Dobbs et al., 2011). The remaining 500 generated an estimated US$30 trillion.

And these numbers are only expected to grow as the share of urbanized population keeps rising. According to Oxford Economics' estimates, **the top 750 most productive cities will contribute close to US$80 trillion to the global GDP by 2030** in 2012 prices (Oxford Economics, 2014, see Figure 2.) Although cities in lower and middle-income countries are estimated to contribute less to global GDP than cities in high-income countries, the expected **individual GDP growth of developing cities is estimated to be higher.**

Figure 2: Cities' contribution to global GDP (%), 2012-2030

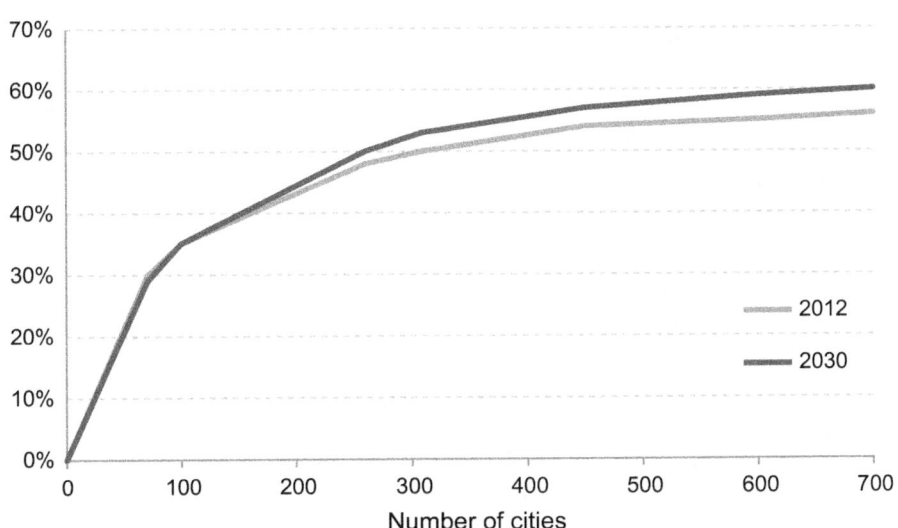

Source: Based on LSE Cities (Floater et al., 2014).
Note: Cities are understood as metropolitan areas of more than 0.5 million people.

---

[2] Measured by expected contribution to global GDP growth by 2025 from 2007.

Chapter 2: Urban Economic Trends and Challenges

A good way to illustrate the increasing economic importance of cities in the global economy is to compare top cities' economic output with large nation-states in terms of GDP and leading multinational corporations' annual revenues, as exhibited in Table 1. **Many cities are among the world's top 100 economies.** In particular, for the year 2014, 42 cities (metropolitan areas) are included in the world's 100 largest economic entities, along with countries and corporations.

Table 1: The world's top 100 economies, 2014 ($ billion PPP)

	Country/Metro City/Corporation	GDP/Revenue		Country/Metro City/Corporation	GDP/Revenue		Country/Metro City/Corporation	GDP/Revenue
1	China	17,188.7	35	Osaka/Kobe	638.2	69	Tianjin	353.5
2	United States	16,490.2	36	Colombia	607.7	70	Singapore	347.8
3	India	6,983.8	37	United Arab Emirates	586.6	71	Nagoya	345.8
4	Japan	4,524.3	38	Shanghai	564.7	72	Shenzhen	345.3
5	Russia	3,633.8	39	Chicago	535.4	73	Boston	342.3
6	Germany	3,523.0	40	Algeria	527.7	74	Istanbul	331.5
7	Brazil	3,124.6	41	Moscow	526.0	75	Norway	329.6
8	Indonesia	2,552.5	42	Venezuela	514.7	76	Philadelphia	329.4
9	France	2,463.9	43	Iraq	500.1	77	Suzhou	322.3
10	United Kingdom	2,460.8	44	Vietnam	487.2	78	San Francisco	314.7
11	Mexico	2,044.0	45	Beijing	481.1	79	PetroChina	312.3
12	Italy	2,026.8	46	Bangladesh	473.9	80	Taipei	311.1
13	Korea	1,696.2	47	Köln-Düsseldorf	461.3	81	Jakarta	305.4
14	Tokyo	1,536.9	48	Houston	459.4	82	Rotterdam-Amsterdam	304.8
15	Saudi Arabia	1,532.6	49	Belgium	458.0	83	Czech Republic	301.8
16	Canada	1,521.3	50	Wal-mart Stores	453.0	84	Buenos Aires	300.3
17	Spain	1,475.8	51	Switzerland	452.6	85	Chongqing	300.0

Country/Metro City/Corporation	GDP/Revenue	Country/Metro City/Corporation	GDP/Revenue	Country/Metro City/Corporation	GDP/Revenue
18 Turkey	1,434.2	52 Royal Dutch Shell	429.1	86 Milan	296.7
19 New York	1,334.2	53 Sweden	426.4	87 Qatar	292.0
20 Iran	1,290.0	54 China Petroleum	423.3	88 Bangkok	291.7
21 Australia	1,015.2	55 Kazakhstan	422.2	89 Busan-Ulsan	281.9
22 Thailand	1,014.3	56 Washington D.C.	420.4	90 Atlanta	279.9
23 Nigeria	1,000.9	57 Sao Paulo	409.3	91 Delhi	279.1
24 Poland	910.5	58 Hong Kong	395.5	92 Portugal	272.2
25 Egypt	900.1	59 Dallas	392.3	93 Greece	267.1
26 Pakistan	849.4	60 Chile	389.4	94 Toronto	262.7
27 Los Angeles	818.0	61 Mexico City	383.7	95 Kuwait	262.3
28 Seoul	804.2	62 Romania	380.9	96 Israel	259.0
29 London	794.4	63 Austria	374.7	97 Seattle	254.2
30 Netherlands	770.1	64 Exxon Mobil	374.6	98 Miami	249.7
31 Malaysia	731.4	65 Guangzhou	361.5	99 Madrid	249.4
32 Paris	679.8	66 British Petroleum	360.5	100 Volkswagen Group	248.6
33 South Africa	672.3	67 Peru	354.7		
34 Philippines	659.1	68 Ukraine	354.3		

Legend: ■ Country; ■ **Metropolitan City;** ■ *Company*.

Source: Own based on (Toly and Tabory, 2016) from World Bank World Development Indicator Series, Brookings Institution Global Metro Monitor 2014, and Forbes Global 2000 List 2014.

Note 1: National and metropolitan GDP figures are at purchasing power parity rates (PPP).

Note 2: The table is intended for illustrative purposes only, as company revenues are different from GDP.

Sectors of the Urban Economy

The economy of each city comprises different sectors. While each sector has its own specificities, some cities are more specialized in some sets of interrelated sectors than others. As a result, some cities' economies are structurally very diverse, while others have more specific "economic profiles," and are dominated by certain areas of the economy. (See Figure 3.)

Figure 3. Gross Value Added (GVA) by sector in selected cities, 2015 (% of total GVA)

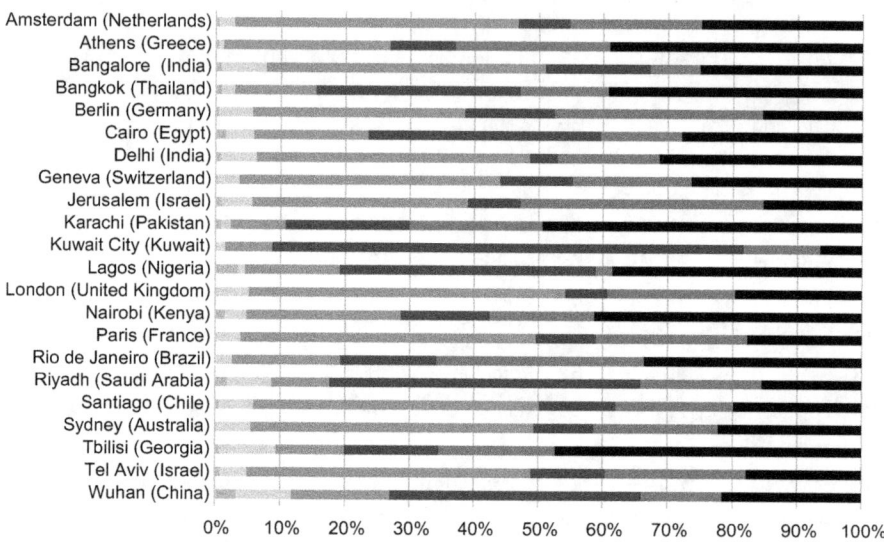

- GVA from Agriculture, Hunting, Forestry and Fishing
- GVA from Construction
- GVA from Financial Intermediation, Real Estate, Renting and Business Activities
- GVA from Mining and Quarrying; Manufacturing; Electricity, Gas and Water Supply
- GVA from Public Administration and Defence; Education; Health; Community, Social and Personal Service Activities; Other Activities
- GVA from Wholesale and Retail Trade; Repair of Motor Vehicles, Personal and Household Goods; Hotels and Restaurants; Transport, Storage and Communications

Source: Own calculations based on Euromonitor International from national statistics (2016).
Note: Cities correspond to metropolitan areas.

Understanding the industry structure and sectors profile of a city is very important, since this helps identify options for economic development and areas of strength. For instance, Figure 3 shows that some cities such as London, Paris, Santiago and Tel Aviv generated more than the 40% of their Gross Value Added (GVA) in 2015 from the "Financial Intermediation, Real Estate, Renting and Business Activities." Meanwhile, other cities such Kuwait City or Riyadh have a very different economic profile with more than 40% of their GVA coming from the "Mining and Quarrying; Manufacturing; Electricity, Gas and Water Supply" sectors. Other urban areas have diverse profiles, with more service-oriented economies. For instance, Jerusalem, Rio de Janeiro and Berlin generated more than 30% of their GVA in 2015 in the "Public Administration and Defense; Education; Health; Community, Social and Personal Service Activities."

Therefore, **each urban area has a different economic identity**. To promote economic development in cities, it is useful to understand their distinct economic profiles and identify which sectors are contributing the most to economic growth, local incomes and employment creation, as well as which ones are more likely to grow in the future. This way city managers can identify new opportunities, develop and promote links and interactions between the different local and regional economic sectors, and promote overall economic growth.

Household Incomes and Emerging Economies

Along with cities' GDP growth, **incomes per capita levels in urban areas are also increasing.** In fact, the positive correlation between the rate of urbanization of a country and its per capita income has been widely studied (Duranton, 2014). According to some estimates, the top 10% of the 750 world's largest cities increased the average disposable income of their households by 9.8 annually from 2005 to 2012 (Kilroy et al., 2015). Even more relevant is that more than two-thirds of the fastest-growing cities in GDP per capita terms were lower-middle-income cities.

The planet will soon experience one of the largest increases in middle-class populations in history, which is described as a key megatrend that will shape governments and social structures in cities around the world. By 2030, the top 750 biggest cities will gain some 220 million additional middle-class consumers, who will boost total global spending and account for some 80% of global consumption (Dobbs et al., 2016; Oxford Economics, 2014).

Most of these new middle-class consumers are expected to originate in cities in emerging economies. By 2025, many of the urban hubs currently ranked among the world's wealthiest cities may no longer make the list of the top 600 in terms of GDP. Meanwhile, more than 100 new cities from developing countries such as China, the Democratic Republic of Congo, Nigeria, Indonesia, Pakistan and India, are expected to make it onto the list for the first time and replace cities from the developed world (UNEP, 2013). The middle class in China, for instance, lives mostly in urban areas and by 2030 could reach one billion people, which is equivalent to 70% of China's projected population (UN-Habitat, 2016).

Emerging cities in the developing world face some of the toughest challenges regarding rapid urbanization, such as shortage of housing and issues of poverty and crime, but they will also account for most of the global income growth. Their own nascent middle class will play an increasingly critical role in the global economy. As stated by a study by the MGI, **only around 440 cities in emerging markets are expected to generate nearly 50% of global GDP growth between 2010 and 2025** (Dobbs et al., 2012). China will lead this GDP growth with 242 cities in these 440 emerging cities; Latin America will follow with 57 cities; South Asia will have 36 cities; and Africa and the Middle East together 39 cities. The balance of economic power held by cities will therefore move swiftly eastward, predominantly toward China. In a study by Oxford Economics, it is estimated that seven out of the top 10 cities with the biggest increase in GDP change by 2030 will be located in China (Oxford Economics, 2014). (See Table 2.)

Table 2. Top 10 cities with the biggest increase in GDP change by 2030 (2013-2030, in US$ billions, 2012 prices)

World rank (2030)	City (Country)	US$ bn (2012 prices)
1	New York-Newark-Jersey City (US)	874
2	Shanghai (China)	734
3	Tianjin (China)	625
4	Beijing (China)	594
5	Los Angeles-Long Beach-Anaheim (US)	522
6	Guangzhou-Guangdong (China)	510
7	Shenzhen (China)	508
8	London-Metro (UK)	476
9	Chongqing (China)	432
10	Suzhou, Jiangsu (China)	394

Source: Oxford Economics (2014)

However, developing and emerging cities still have a long way to go before they catch up with developed cities. Closing the gaps in living standards and wages between developed and developing countries will still take decades. Cities in developing countries face greater and more complex challenges than more industrialized countries. They are still struggling to develop basic infrastructure that enables economic prosperity, such as basic housing and sanitation. As a consequence, they need substantial physical capital investments. However, in many cases, they do not have the financial tools required for these huge investments. **The funding gap between emerging and developed cities is still very high.** Those cities that are able to find solutions to finance their infrastructure needs will be the ones that will be able to foster economic growth and will play a more relevant role in the future global economy.

Rising Inequalities

Expanding urbanization along with increasing GDPs has helped millions of people escape poverty in recent decades. We have moved from 1.9 billion people living in extreme poverty (on less than US$1.90 a day) in 1990 to some 900 million people in 2012, and expecting a decline to 702 million in 2015 (less than 10% of total population) (UN-Habitat, 2016). However, the influx of rural poor into cities, especially in developing countries, has created important **hubs of urban poverty. Around one-third of the urban population in developing countries lives in slum conditions**.

A slum in Manila (Philippines)

Source: Pixabay, CC0

Additionally, despite rising GDPs per capita, we also find a greater polarization of those incomes. The world has experienced important economic growth in recent decades, but one that has not been shared and allocated equitably. Today, the world is more unequal than some decades ago. And these widening income gaps and rising inequality are often concentrated and aggravated in cities. In fact, according to some estimates, **75% of the world's cities have higher levels of income inequality today compared with 20 years ago** (UN-Habitat, 2016).

These high levels of urban poverty and increasing intra-urban inequalities have become an important policy issue in cities around the world because **poverty exacerbates problems of social exclusion** in cities, such as unequal access to health services, education and opportunities to some groups of the society. Although these issues are going to be analyzed in more detail in the book volume *Cities and Social Cohesion*, it is important to also briefly mention them here because **poverty and economic inequality are jeopardizing the potential economic benefits brought by urbanization**. Urban leaders need to implement policies and regulations that ensure both social and economic growth, while helping reduce inequalities.

Informal Economy

A significant proportion of the economy in many cities all over the world, especially in developing countries, is generated by the informal economy or the informal sector. The informal economy refers to those economic activities, enterprises, jobs and workers that are not regulated, registered or protected by the state or by any form of government. As a result, they are not taxed and they do not appear in official economic data or in national production calculations.

The issue of the informal economy is important because it is linked to weaker protection of working conditions (see next section 2.2), lower productivity, and reduces the base for public revenues. Consequently, cities with a large informal sector must try to integrate the informal sector into the formal market to exploit the full economic potential of their cities and improve the quality of life of their citizens.

According to estimates, **in developing countries in Asia and Africa, the informal economy accounts for 25% to 40% of GDP** (UN-Habitat, 2016). Since the urban informal sector tends to be inaccurately measured in national GDP and income calculations, especially in lower income countries, the percentage of national economies corresponding to urban areas might be underestimated.

***

2.2 Employment Generation

People move to cities looking for more and better employment opportunities, economic prospects and, eventually, a better life for themselves and their families. In general, being employed, earning a decent income and having good working conditions are essential for a person's well-being. And urban areas often provide more employment opportunities than rural areas. According to some estimates, cities create jobs four to five times faster (Kilroy et al., 2015). More precisely, private sector jobs accounted for most of this job growth. The World Bank estimates that, between 2006 and 2012, the 750 largest cities in the world generated 87.7 million private sector jobs, which is equivalent to 58% of all new private sector jobs in those 129 countries (Fikri and Zhu, 2015). Thus, **urban areas are key engines of employment creation in nations around the world.**

As more and more people move to cities and urban populations grow, we find an increasing number of people trying to enter the job market in urban areas, which results in a booming demand for employment opportunities in cities. However, there is a great variability between cities in their ability to create jobs. For instance, from 2005 to 2012, the top 10% of the world's largest cities achieved 9.2% annual jobs growth, compared with 1.9% that was created in the other 90% of cities (Kilroy et al., 2015).

Thus, many cities around the world are not able to cope with this growing demand for urban jobs, which often results in high unemployment rates. In fact, cities are often considered centers of high unemployment, which is known as the *urban paradox:* **cities offer more employment opportunities, but they are also frequently characterized by higher unemployment rates, inequality, and social exclusion, with extremes of wealth and poverty** (UN-Habitat, 2016). This appears to be one of the most common trade-offs of city economies.

Unemployment

Most cities are often distinguished by both highly productive districts or neighborhoods and isolated groups or areas of very high unemployment (OECD, 2015). For instance, about 60% of unemployment in the UK, Japan, Korea, Netherlands and the US is concentrated in urban areas (UN-Habitat, 2016). In 2015, the global unemployment rate stood at some 6%, reaching 197.1 million people, which is 0.7 million more than in 2014 (ILO, 2016b).

Employment in cities is a critical issue for several reasons. First, without employment there are no incomes for people or companies in order to invest and improve their living conditions and well-being (Cohen, 2015). Second, public revenues depend partly on employment taxes, money that is needed to invest in public services and infrastructure. Third, participation in the labor market is a critical indicator of social inclusion since it is one of the clearest examples of the intrinsically linked "social" and "economic" aspects of exclusion.

Table 3. Selected cities with high unemployment rates (% of economically active population)

City (Country)	Unemployment rate 2015
Nairobi (Kenya)	42.0
Skopje (Macedonia)	27.9
Athens (Greece)	26.1
Sarajevo (Bosnia-Herzegovina)	24.8
Tbilisi (Georgia)	20.8
Johannesburg (South Africa)	19.5
Barcelona (Spain)	19.5
Cape Town (South Africa)	18.8
Belgrade (Serbia)	17.2
Madrid (Spain)	16.8

Source: Euromonitor International from International Labour Organisation (ILO)/Eurostat/national statistics/OECD

Long-term unemployment has very important negative financial and social effects on personal life and social cohesion and it is a critical factor in people being at risk of exclusion and poverty. Unemployment impacts population groups differently, with some groups of society more vulnerable than others. Globally, women and youth are more likely to be affected by unemployment, with youth unemployment rates in both developed and developing countries being more than twice that of adults.

Informal Employment

Another key challenge for local governments is **informality in employment**, which has been mentioned in the previous section and that particularly affects developing countries. In African cities, the majority of jobs are in the informal sector, with less than 25% of new workers entering the labor market and wage employment. In the city of Kampala (Uganda), for instance, 57.3% of all jobs are in the informal sector (Lall, 2016). Another example is in India, where almost 80% of their labor force is employed in the informal sector (Cohen, 2015). Women and migrants are the most vulnerable groups to be excluded from formal employment, since they usually have low-level skills, and they are the most likely to end up taking informal low-quality jobs. In addition, in developing countries there is a risk of child labor exploitation.

Highlighting informal employment is important because, although it is difficult to generalize its quality, it often leads to weaker protection for workers, poor employment conditions and increasing poverty. Poor employment conditions include the absence of safeguards in the occurrence of non-payment of wages, compulsory overtime, lack of social benefits and unsafe environments (ILO, 2016a). Therefore, the integration of informal workers into the formal labor market is a key challenge that must be addressed by city governments around the world, especially in developing countries.

All in all, **reducing unemployment rates and informal employment should be a priority for city leaders around the world.** Although local governments are not directly or entirely responsible for generating employment and improving employment conditions, and they cannot implement labor policies, which is carried out by national governments, city leaders can stimulate job creation through different actions and projects, as will be exhibited in Section 3. For instance, in order to facilitate job creation city managers can create the essential conditions to ease businesses and promote entrepreneurship; or improve the health and education systems or infrastructures of a city, all of which contribute to the job market. At the same time, municipal leaders can stimulate job creation, as well as protect the more vulnerable groups of society, by developing social protection mechanisms for the unemployed.

***

2.3 Economic Agglomeration and Urban Productivity

Goods and services are usually produced more efficiently in densely populated areas, where business can find an abundant concentration and availability of workers and skilled labor, together with a critical mass of customers, offering a bigger market size and higher demand. **This abundant concentration of resources allows for agglomeration benefits, economies of scale and clustering effects, increasing productivity and competitiveness.**

Economic agglomeration refers to the benefits, economic efficiencies and positive externalities that firms and individuals obtain by locating near each other. The dense concentration of people and clusters of activity in cities allows for a bigger accumulation of infrastructure and physical capital, which eases resource sharing; offers a larger labor market, which facilitates a quicker and better matching of both workers and skilled labor; and allows for customers and suppliers to be in close proximity, which reduces transport and communication costs. All of these factors allow for knowledge spillovers between firms (both within the same sector and across industries), a faster spread of ideas, more learning for workers, and a more diverse, intellectual, creative and entrepreneurial environment.

Economies of agglomeration in urban areas usually result in increases in productivity. In fact, there is much evidence that supports the **positive effect that agglomeration economies have on productivity and wages in urban areas**. In 2012, 70% of cities of the top 750 largest cities outperformed their countries in terms of productivity (Kilroy et al., 2015). More precisely, larger cities tend to be even more productive than smaller cities. (See Figure 4.)

Chapter 2: Urban Economic Trends and Challenges

Figure 4: Larger metropolitan areas are more productive, 2010

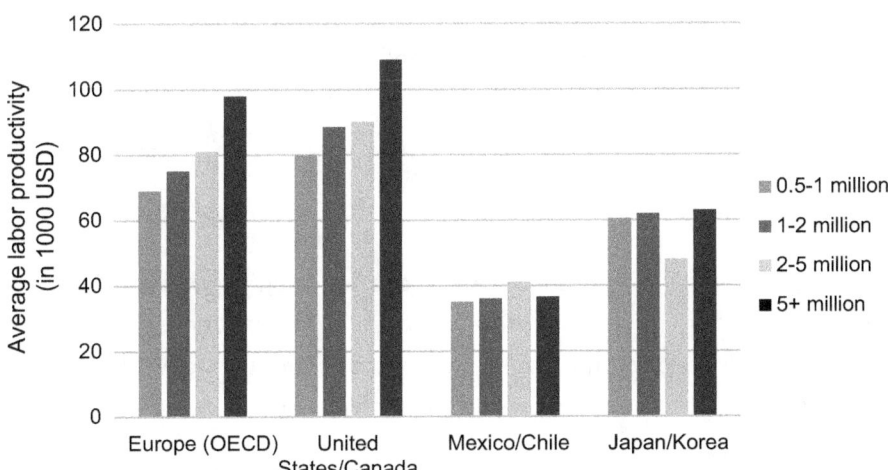

Source: OECD calculations (2015) based on OECD (2014), "Metropolitan areas", OECD Regional Statistics database.
Note: Average labor productivity (USD per year), depending on the size of the metropolitan area.

Some studies suggest that "a city that is 10% larger in population offers wages that are 0.2 to 1% higher." (Duranton, 2014). But such increases in productivity and wages in cities has not always been transferred to workers equally, as we have seen in the previous sections. Also, the effect varies widely between developing countries and developed countries. Therefore, city managers around the world must pay special attention to the drawbacks associated with economies of agglomeration, such as strong competition for resources and jobs, inequalities and the lack of affordable housing, in order to be able to maximize the benefits of agglomeration.

Advances in Information and Communication Technologies (ICTs) are facilitating and enhancing productivity and economic development in cities around the world by enlarging cities' agglomeration advantages and revolutionizing production processes, transport modes and costs, and making larger distances seem much smaller. In fact, **the deployment of ICT**

technologies is disrupting all areas of businesses and across sectors, boosting productivity in cities. Although agglomeration is something that city governments cannot create through policy, they can promote the potential benefits of agglomeration through different actions and initiatives, as we will see in Section 3.

Competitiveness

When a nation, region or city experiences long-run productivity, it often results in what is known as competitiveness. Competitiveness refers to a place where firms operating there are able to compete successfully in the national and global economy, while maintaining or improving wages and living standards for the average citizen.

During the 20th century, competitiveness was mainly studied on a national level. However, since the late 1990s and the beginning of the 2000s, the center of attention has moved to the municipal and regional levels. Therefore, the discussion about **competitiveness has shifted from being a policy area tied solely to nations to a current focus on "urban competitiveness."** Today, urban competitiveness and local economic development have become core issues in local public policy. According to a report by the World Economic Forum, a city's competitiveness can be defined as "the set of factors – policies, institutions, strategies and processes – that determines the level of a city's sustainable productivity" (WEF, 2014).

Many factors can drive and contribute to cities competitiveness: urban infrastructure, business environment, public services, communications, natural resources, social and human capital, among many others. However, not all cities are equally endowed with all of these factors. Some of them are exogenous and beyond the control of urban policymakers, such as natural resources or geographical location. Others, on the other hand, are endogenous and can be influenced by city administrators, such as a good urban economic development strategy, public-private sector cooperation or institutional flexibility. The location-specific context is critical for identifying the main factors that enable growth.

Although cities are still very much subjected to national economic policies, which is itself a challenge, urban managers have many instruments at their disposal for fostering urban competitiveness and economic development, as we will exhibit in Section 3. However, improving a city's competitiveness takes time and it will require all kinds of involved stakeholders to be actively engaged.

***

2.4 A Connected World: Cities as Hubs of the Global Economy

Cities are increasingly interconnected regionally, nationally and globally. New information technologies and networks have made distances seem smaller, enabling the spread of globalization. Indeed, **urbanization and globalization are two of the main major forces shaping the global economy today**. Cities can now operate in global markets for goods, services, finance and, increasingly, even in labor. This offers new possibilities and opportunities for connections around the world, but it also increases the competition at the global stage to attract resources.

In the case of cities, **their ability and capacity to participate in the global economy has become crucial** for the development of their local economies. The current stage of economic globalization has allowed firms to market their goods in distant locations and has facilitated the fragmentation of production chains, creating the so-called Global Value Chains (GVCs).

GVCs have led to the manufacturing of different parts of a single product at diverse locations around the world. Cities must be well integrated in these GVCs through trade, direct and indirect foreign investment (FDI), tourism and foreign talent, in order to be nodal points of GVCs and become primary hubs of the global economy (WEF, 2016). Additionally, irreversible trends such as technological revolution and digitalization have made connectivity and mutual interdependence among urban hubs easier and more relevant than ever before. As a result, **in today's increasingly globalized and hyperconnected world, cities must re-emerge as strategic global centers for specialized functions, and as hubs of trade, movements of people, capital and information.**

However, globalization also strengthens certain advantages of proximity, such as face-to-face communications and a high concentration of infrastructure and resources, which contributes at the same time to further urbanization (World Bank, 2000). For instance, the concentration of physical infrastructures in cities, such as roads, airports and ports, brings benefits to urban areas because they are better connected on our globalized planet. In fact, one of the paradoxes of today's world is that, even though the costs of connecting across long distances have decreased notably, the advantages of urban proximity have become even more valuable than ever before (The Economist, 2014).

Although many firms now work and serve internationally, they still need to have a headquarters (HQ) from where they operate globally to serve a larger economy. And cities are the links in global networks of multinational corporations (MNCs). The more globalized and digitalized a company is, the more complex its central HQ functions will be, and the more they will take advantage from densely resource–rich urban environments (Sassen, 2008). As a result, urban centers compete to host multinational or regional enterprises HQ and to be nodal points of GVCs and attract FDI.

According to the McKinsey Global Institute (MGI), only 20 cities are home to more than one-third of all large companies (i.e. at least $1 billion in annual revenues), accounting for 40% of the revenue of all large companies (Dobbs et al., 2013). **Headquarters are therefore a good indicator of cities' global influence and can be a defining characteristic of urban economic power.** (See Table 4.)

Table 4: Cities by number of headquarters (2012)

Rank	City	Country	# HQs	Rank	City	Country	# HQs
1	Tokyo	Japan	154	14	Sydney	Australia	21
2	New York	US	82	15	Moscow	Russia	20
3	London	UK	68	16	Stockholm	Sweden	20
4	Paris	France	60	17	Washington	US	18
5	Seoul	South Korea	60	18	Madrid	Spain	18
6	Hong Kong	China	48	19	San Francisco	US	17
7	Beijing	China	45	20	Zurich	Switzerland	16
8	Chicago	US	31	21	Minneapolis	US	14
9	Houston	US	27	22	Munich	Germany	9
10	Mumbai	India	26	23	Rio de Janeiro	Brazil	7
11	San Jose	US	25	24	Frankfurt	Germany	6
12	Toronto	Canada	23	25	The Hague	Netherlands	3
13	Dallas	US	21				

Source: GaWC (Csomos, 2013)

Note: Cities correspond to metropolitan areas and number of headquarters refers to the number of headquarters of publicly traded companies.

Traditional global hubs like Tokyo, New York or London are situated in the top positions of the ranking, but as a result of global restructuring, some cities in emerging countries, such as Beijing, Mumbai, Moscow and Rio de Janeiro are also becoming leading cities of the global economy (Csomos, 2013).

Cities can translate their strategic position in global trade flows into an economic opportunity. A key challenge for city managers around the world is to understand the role of their local companies in international networks to strength their positions, as well as to attract investment that is in line with the city's characteristics and competitive advantage.

Despite all the opportunities, globalization also entails risks, since global connectivity makes cities more vulnerable to regional and global dynamics, international changes and international competition, by exposing countries to greater risks of contagion from crises. The 2008 global financial crisis is a good example of the domino effect of global economic connectivity. In fact, economy recovery after the crisis has been slow and some regions across the globe are still experiencing economic crises.

***

3. Cities as Enablers of Sustainable Economic Prosperity: Smart Solutions and Best Practices

Balancing economic advantages with the challenges posed by rapid urbanization is one of the major dilemmas faced by city managers and policymakers around the world. Cities not only have to seek economic growth, but economic growth that is sustainable over time. A successful vision of urban economic growth should consider three key aspects: productivity and competitiveness (i.e. economic development), inclusivity (i.e. social development) and resiliency (i.e. based on sustainable environmental development).

As mentioned in other volumes of this series, a number of leverages of change are enabling groundbreaking transformations in the way cities operate and grow. At IESE Cities in Motion, we have defined a framework of analysis with these main leverages of change to help us understand and analyze how they interact between each other in the different solutions. The overall framework is presented in Figure 5.

Chapter 3: Cities as Enablers of Sustainable Economic Prosperity

Figure 5. Smart urban management model

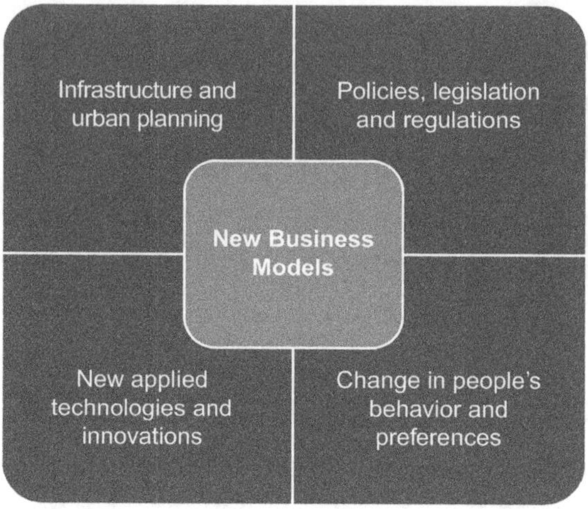

```
┌─────────────────────────┬─────────────────────────┐
│  Infrastructure and     │  Policies, legislation  │
│  urban planning         │  and regulations        │
│                         │                         │
│            ┌────────────────────────┐             │
│            │    New Business        │             │
│            │    Models              │             │
│            └────────────────────────┘             │
│                         │                         │
│  New applied            │  Change in people's     │
│  technologies and       │  behavior and           │
│  innovations            │  preferences            │
└─────────────────────────┴─────────────────────────┘
```

Source: Prepared by the authors.

In the case of the economy, these key forces are playing a critical role in facilitating employment creation, economic growth and rising incomes. First, technological breakthroughs and innovations in general, and digital transformation in particular, are changing how enterprises operate and trade, and altering the way people work and how they access and buy products. Technological advances are disrupting all areas of businesses in the economy, and across sectors, giving rise to new business models and new sectors within urban economies. Also, these new business models can help city leaders gather more accurate information about the current situation of their cities and deliver better urban services. Cities need to embrace these technological advances and new business models to adapt and transform themselves to the new realities.

In fact, new applied technologies are revolutionizing consumer behavior and preferences, which is the second leverage of change in the model. People's preferences and behaviors are changing, especially in the case of younger generations, who are looking for different ways of consuming and new production models. This shift in consumers' preferences is enabling the rise of new economies, such the *collaborative economy*, the *circular economy* and the *green economy*. City leaders should facilitate the transformation into these new urban economies to adapt to current dynamics of change and new urban realities.

Third, institutions, regulations and legislations are also key elements for competitiveness and economic development. Through different regulations and legislations reforms, city governments can create a thriving business climate and investment environment. City leaders face the challenge of legislating policies and smart regulations that can create jobs at the local level and position local firms to compete in the global market place. Despite the fact that city governments cannot "create" an economy by themselves, they can be enablers of economic development through the regulatory system of a city. Therefore, a commitment from the public sector to develop trust and shape smart regulations, linking urban policies to economic development, is crucial to enhance competitiveness and improve the quality of life of citizens.

Finally, good infrastructure, land and urban planning are also critical factors for a city's economy. Since the conditions of a city's infrastructure affects the cost of production and functioning of many different economic activities, an inadequate urban infrastructure, both physical and digital, can hinder economic growth if resources are not optimally allocated. A well-planned and integrated urban system is key for achieving local economic development.

Building cities that are engines of economic growth - but inclusive, safe, resilient and sustainable at the same time - requires effective strategic policy choices and adequate investments. Both national and local governments play an important role in building the economic development of the cities of the future. More precisely, local managers have a great capacity to influence the economic outcome of their cities through different strategic plans and policies. Cities can facilitate job creation, raise productivity and increase incomes per capita through different initiatives, plans or policies, such as: local economic development action plans, improving the entrepreneurial ecosystem, creating sustainable economic districts, clustering, innovation initiatives, attraction of talent, the promotion of contacts among related industries and firms, among others, as it will be exhibited in this section. However, it is important to mention that the context and dynamics of each individual city are unique, thus the challenges they must overcome to succeed are also diverse. There is no single recipe for positive economic development in cities. Every city leader must analyze the weakness and strengths of their own city and prioritize the most important factors.

However, some common elements or patterns can be identified, and cities can learn from each other when designing and implementing economic development plans and strategies. This section presents a number of insightful examples, initiatives and best practices regarding local economic development that have proven to be successful in cities around the world. First of all, the key role of infrastructure and urban services as drivers of city's competitiveness will be emphasized. Second, the importance of creating a good business climate and a good legal and regulatory environment for competitiveness, innovation and entrepreneurship will also be examined. And lastly, the relevance of being able to keep up with economic transformations and new urban economies is going to be analyzed.

***

3.1 Infrastructure and Urban Services

To grow, a city must work well. When urban services and infrastructures are not able to keep up with the pace of a growing population, it results in a suboptimal allocation of resources and an inefficient management of the city, which can hinder economic growth. Cities must be able to deliver, on one hand, **efficient "physical" urban services** for citizens, such as infrastructure, efficient mobility and transportation systems, water, waste management, energy, residential and commercial buildings, etc.[3]; and on the other hand, they must also provide **"soft" urban services**, such as a good healthcare system, education system, security, communications, law and legislation, broadband connectivity, culture, etc.[4]

Cities must take advantage of their strategic location and the fact that **most public intervention, public services and infrastructure are concentrated in urban areas**. In cities and their metropolitan areas are concentrated most of the global physical infrastructures, such as roads, bridges, airports and ports, as well as water supply, sewers systems, electrical grids, telecommunications and land. All of these elements play a crucial role in enabling economic development, facilitating access to jobs and amenities, and improving a city's energy efficiency. City managers should plan a city's physical infrastructure and public services in an integrated way, so as to improve the economic environment of the city; facilitate the access to people, knowledge and capital; enable good living conditions for citizens and firms; and to connect local territories to a globalized economy, which is essential in a multi-connected world.

---

[3] The issues of physical urban services are covered more in detail in other volumes of the series such as *Cities and Mobility & Transportation* and *Cities and the Environment*, and are going to be further develop in the book *Cities and Urban Planning*.

[4] Issues of education are going to be analyzed in the volume *Cities and Human Capital*; issues of security and healthcare in *Cities and Social Cohesion*; and the topic of connectivity and communications in *Cities and Technology*.

For instance, by developing transportation and communications infrastructures, city governments could facilitate the movement of goods, employees, customers and suppliers, both within the city and with its metropolitan areas. A good example of this is the introduction of a public mass transit cable car system in the city of Medellin (Colombia), which allowed access to jobs and facilities to the inner city to previously marginalized communities in the surrounding areas. The cable car improved employees' quality of life going to work and moved customers closer to suppliers.[5] Another example in the field of transportation and communications infrastructures is the improvement of the old Tangier's port. The Moroccan city decided to create a new port with greater capacity to accommodate larger container ships to improve economic conditions in the city. Now, Tangier's port is one of the largest intermodal facilities on the Mediterranean Coast and Africa's biggest container port (Kilroy et al., 2015). This has created economic opportunities for local companies and has facilitated local economic development.

Old Tangier's port (Morocco)

Source: Pixabay, CC0

[5] To know more on this case study, see *Cities and Mobility & Transportation*.

Another important issue is the **improvement of web connectivity and ICT networks**, which plays a very important role in creating an attractive urban environment, being able to provide the right information for business, and improves quality of life. This is especially important in cities in developing countries, where sometimes the ICT infrastructure barrier is too high for new businesses to develop in today's hyperconnected world. However, some cities and countries in the developing world are improving their connectivity infrastructures, which is creating important economic opportunities. Cities like Lagos in Nigeria and Bangalore in India are becoming "technology hubs" in their regions with important entrepreneurs and innovators in these sectors, thanks to expansions in internet access and connectivity at the city level (Deloitte, 2014).

Therefore, city managers should work on providing all these urban services and urban infrastructures in the most efficient way possible, adapting the strategic plan to the specific urban reality and prioritizing in the city's major deficits. This requires the involvement of a large number of stakeholders in the planning and administrative process of delivering urban services, including governments, citizens, the private sector and NGOs. The creation of a **platform of collaboration** between the public and private sectors, through different forms of Public-Private Partnerships (PPPs), can be a good way to create and develop those infrastructures and urban services.

***

3.2 A Good Business Environment for Competitiveness

In a challenging and competitive economic global climate, having a culture of innovation and entrepreneurship is critical for cities to succeed. **Creating a favorable business climate involves government administrations at local, regional and national levels.** However, cities can also implement many initiatives and regulations to create the right conditions to foster business innovation, making it easier for established companies to run their daily operations, attract investment and provide a positive environment for new business, start-ups and entrepreneurs to launch, grow and expand.

In this section, we are going to discuss some of the policies, instruments, actions and programs that city governments have at their disposal to enhance the business environment of a city and improve its competitiveness. These include: developing favorable regulations to ease doing business (3.2.1); creating a favorable entrepreneurial ecosystem (3.2.2); fostering innovation and creativity at all levels and across all sectors of the economy (3.2.3); and implementing different diversification and competitiveness policies, such as industry clustering (3.2.4). These policies and strategies cannot be implemented overnight – instead they form part of a long-term process. But if urban leaders have a clear vision of their long-term objectives regarding local economic development, they can be important actors for enhancing and fostering a dynamic economic environment in their cities.

3.2.1 Ease of Doing Business

Enterprises and entrepreneurs are the main drivers of economic growth and economic development. But city authorities are the ones that determine how these businesses are regulated. If cities want to exploit the benefits of agglomeration and take a leading role in stimulating economic growth and job creation, **local governments must provide a favorable environment for business**.

In addition to direct instruments such as public funds or public loans, as we will see in upcoming sections, city managers can also support local economic development by providing the "soft" infrastructure needed to create, run and grow businesses. They can create favorable regulations or laws to provide an attractive, well-functioning and efficient local business environment. Possible actions include modifying the tax regime; easing the access to capital and financing; creating simple and transparent regulations and administrative processes; developing trade policies that encourage foreign investment; smoothing visa and immigration processes; easing employee mobility; and/or ensuring intellectual property (IP) protection and anti-trust laws.

One approach is to remove tax on capital gains and dividends from long-term equity investments in the city that employ a minimum percentage of city residents (Porter, 1995). Another possible way to improve the regulatory environment is to offer one-stop shopping for business permits for urban entrepreneurs, instead of having to deal with multiple and diverse agencies (Glaeser, 2015). The *Devens Enterprise Commission*, in Devens, Massachusetts (USA), is an example of this model. However, it is important to stress that this does not mean abruptly deregulating markets. Nor is it suggested that by reducing the cost of doing business, economic development will automatically happen. The goal is to create a positive business environment adapted to local conditions and to implement smart regulations that address the latest business models and technologies.

BOX 1: Kigali, facilitation of doing business

Kigali is the capital and largest city of Rwanda with a population of more than 1 million people. It has been the economic and political center of the country since its independence in 1962. With a GDP per capita of US$1,380 in 2012, it falls into the category of a low-income city (Kulenovic and Cech, 2015). Kigali's economy is in the process of rebuilding. Largely preindustrial, the most important sectors of the economy are tourism, construction and non-tradable goods.

In order to improve the business environment, the city leaders of Kigali created a private sector forum, the Kigali Investors' Forum. The goal was to initiate a public-private collaboration to identify specific reforms needed (Kilroy et al., 2015). Forum members identified the inefficiency and lack of coordination of construction permits as an important constraint in doing business. Before the reform, businesses needed 125 days to receive a construction permit (Kulenovic and Cech, 2015). To solve this problem, they decided to establish a One-Stop Shop in 2010 to reduce administration processes and in 2011, they also created an electronic platform for construction permits (Kilroy et al., 2015). Investors can now carry out all approval processes in one place and today it only takes 30 days to get a construction permit.

Kigali's business reform is a good example of how the private and the public sectors can work together to improve the business climate of a city and ease procedures for local businesses.

Kigali, Rwanda

Source: Flickr/oledoe.

3.2.2 Entrepreneurship

Entrepreneurship and innovation are two of the most powerful forces boosting local economic development, long-term sustainable growth, productivity and jobs creation in cities and countries around the world.[6] Entrepreneurs produce new products, services and ideas. They also provide jobs and incomes not only for themselves, but also for other citizens. In fact, **entrepreneurial activity is highly related to economic growth and prosperity**.

Entrepreneurs and small and medium enterprises (hereinafter SMEs) will locate their businesses where they find proximity to suppliers and customers; to people and potential employees; to ideas, knowledge and technology flows; and to good infrastructures and capital; all elements that are usually found more abundantly in urban areas.

However, a diverse range of other factors can also influence and facilitate the formation and rise of entrepreneurs and SMEs. While city authorities cannot develop business by themselves or create communities of entrepreneurs, they can design better conditions for entrepreneurs and SMEs to flourish, as well as implement policies and regulations that encourage local entrepreneurial cultures. Some of these better conditions or regulations have been mentioned in the previous sections, such as: a good connective infrastructure, institutional characteristics, and basic urban services; favorable regulatory and legal frameworks; specialized business infrastructures; or the possibility to access to both financial capital and human capital. Indeed, some studies suggest that, within a given city, **entrepreneurs are more likely to establish and/or expand a business in a favorable regulatory and financial environment** (Gonzales Rocha, 2012).

---

[6] This section will look at the issue of entrepreneurship and next section will focus on innovation.

Therefore, implementing measures and programs to improve the entrepreneurial ecosystem of a city is vital for fostering local economic development. These **measures should address market failures and problems usually faced by entrepreneurs and start-up companies**, such as limited supply to finance, business development services, education and training, or facilitating the access to information. This can be done indirectly by creating a good business and entrepreneurial climate, or directly, by providing entrepreneurship courses and education; creating training and mentorship networks for SMEs; or giving subsidies or targeted tax breaks to promote entrepreneurship, such as public funds, public loans or other kinds of financial support.

> Change in people's behavior and preferences

> Policies, legislation and regulations

BEST PRACTICE: SEOUL
Youth 1,000 CEO Project

Seoul is the capital and the largest city of South Korea, with a population of over 10 million people covering 605 km². The metropolitan area hosts more than 25 million inhabitants. Today, Seoul is the business and financial hub of South Korea and a leading and rising global city. As of 2014, the city's GDP was US$846 billion (metro) and a GDP per capita of over US$35,000. With high-growth potential, Seoul is Asia's 4th largest economy and the world's 15th.

Seoul, South Korea

Source: Pixabay, CC0.

Context

- In the late 1990s, an important financial crisis in Asia resulted in the closure of many companies and widespread unemployment.

- The *chaebols,* a South Korean form of business conglomerate, were at the center of South Korea's development policy, and therefore a preferred career choice for young workers. The crisis resulted in the collapse of 11 of South Korea's 30 largest *chaebols* (Watson and Freudmann, 2011).

- As many young workers chose to work in *chaebols,* the unemployment affected them to a greater extent. In 2008, the unemployment rate of South Korea stood at 3.2%; 7% for youth in their 20s to 30s (Seoul Solution, 2014). After the 2009 financial crisis, youth unemployment rose to around 8%.

- The crisis provided many incentives for reforms. The government introduced some tax reforms and other regulations and initiatives. However, convincing people to start their own business was still one of the biggest challenges (Watson and Freudmann, 2011).

- The majority of the previous business incubating policies of the city of Seoul focused on older generations.

Actions

- With the aim of tackling youth unemployment, inspiring young entrepreneurs to consider alternatives from joining the conglomerates and increasing young people's enthusiasm for starting their own businesses, the City of Seoul initiated the program "Youth 1,000 CEO project" in 2009.

- The project aimed to motivate young people aged 20-39 to start their own businesses. This is one of the first long-term projects focused on young people.

- The city government invested a huge budget of over 19 billion (KRW) each year in related programs.

- Since the establishment of the program, 1,000 winners have been selected yearly with ideas for new business opportunities. Winners receive grants of up to 1 million won per month, free office space for founding a business, as well as other support including training, consulting and marketing services.

- The program gives an extra advantage to women, the disabled, previous contest winners and those who have recently failed in setting up a business and are trying again (Ramirez and Youn-joo, 2012). Therefore, besides encouraging entrepreneurship, the initiative also aims to be socially inclusive.

- Lastly, the city has also introduced the "Youth Business Curator Center," in areas both north and south of the Han River. Each center accommodates up to 1,000 people. A task force is responsible for supporting start-up companies in the Seoul Business Agency (SBA) (Seoul Solution, 2014).

Outcomes

- The program has been two or three times more successful than initially expected (Ramirez and Youn-joo, 2012).

- According to a program official, the profit ratio per investment is positive with new businesses' average profit around 300 billion won (KRW), and resulting in two or three people who earned 10 billion (KRW) won each (Seoul Solution, 2014).

- The project is estimated to have generated 5,892 jobs in its first year. As of October 2011, the youth enterprises introduced by the "Youth Business 1000" program had employed 11,221 people and created some 1,500 new youth enterprises (Ramirez and Youn-joo, 2012; Seoul Solution, 2014).

- Initial assistance and support for start-ups, especially in the first phase of the project, has proven to be very effective.

SMEs

SMEs frequently account for the largest proportion of any city's employment. Their contribution to employment is especially high in the case of low-income and middle-income countries and cities. In the formal sector, SMEs provide two-thirds of formal sector jobs in developing countries and up to 80% in low-income countries (Cohen, 2015). Additionally, they not only provide employment to the largest number of people, they also create the greatest number of new jobs across country income groups (Demirgüç-Kunt, 2011).

As a result of the critical importance of SMEs for local economic development and employment, city managers should prioritize the promotion of both entrepreneurship and SMEs as a top issue in their local economic development plans and employment strategies.

Chapter 3: Cities as Enablers of Sustainable Economic Prosperity

> Policies, legislation and regulations

BEST PRACTICE: GLIWICE (POLAND)
Fostering and financing innovative SMEs

The city of Gliwice, located in the Southeastern part of Poland, is the second largest city in the Upper Silesian old-industrialized mining region with a population of some 190,000 inhabitants in some 133 km². Gliwice is one of the cities in the urban area known as Katowice. It has a population of 2.7 million and is within the larger Silesian metropolitan area.

Gliwice, Poland

Source: Pixabay, CC0.

Context

- Gliwice has traditionally been a typical industrial and mining city.

- Since the end of the Socialist period in 1989, the city has experienced a complex process of transformation. The city had to politically and institutionally restructure itself towards the market economy.

- In the 1990s, some coal mines were closed and the city experienced economic growth based on knowledge-based enterprises, mostly in the technology sector.

- In 1996, the Katowice Special Economic Zone (SEZ)[7] was created with the aim of sustaining economic reconversion and attracting firms through a form of state subsidies offering a total exemption from corporation tax for 10 years and the possibility of maintaining a partial exemption of up to half of the firm's income (Fayman et al., 2011). This created an important advantage for the city's attraction to companies and international investments.

---

[7] See point 3.2.4 to know more about Special Economic Zones (SEZ).

- Small and Medium Enterprises (SMEs) play a critical role in the local economy, representing 99% of total enterprises in Gliwice.

Actions

- Given the high number of SMEs in the city, improving conditions for entrepreneurship, promoting the creation of SMEs and providing them with good services (e.g. financial support, consultancy, etc.) became a crucial policy for the local administration.

- The Regional Strategy of Innovation for the Silesian Voivideship 2003-2013 identified the development of SMEs as one of the main goals of regional innovation development. Additionally, the City of Gliwice developed the "Strategy of Integrated and Sustainable Development of Gliwice to 2020," which supported entrepreneurship among local citizens as a priority.

- To help SMEs, the Gliwice's City Council has been taking on many activities to strengthen entrepreneurship and innovation, and facilitating access to both financial and non-financial support.

- In line with the main goal, the City of Gliwice invited different institutions to collaborate. Many actors were involved in this challenge. First, the municipality managed several programs for SMEs. Second, the Local Development Agency (LDA), provided support through the management of incubators and own training programs. Third, the Academy of Entrepreneurship, together with the Technical University, provided studies in the fields of entrepreneurship, economy, etc. In addition to other infrastructures and education facilities, such as the Technology Park and the Silesian Foundation of Support for Enterprises, were created (Fayman et al., 2011).

- One of the main activities is the entrepreneurship incubator program, a support program for innovative projects and companies, the Science and Technology Park "Gliwice Technopark." The main activity of the park is a creation and promotion of innovative and advanced technology companies and transfer of innovative technologies from the Silesian University of Technology and R+D units to small and medium-sized enterprises. The Technopark has three main objectives: (a) incubation of newly created SMEs; (b) transfer of technology; and (c) promotion of entrepreneurship.

- Moreover, the incubator run by the LDA supports startups with low rents (40% of the building is rented to subsidized enterprises), provides training and advisory assistance, cooperation with other scientists, etc.

- Between 2008 and 2011, Gliwice was part of the Fin-Urb-Act network within the URBACT II, with European funds, created to support local SMEs and innovative economies.

Outcomes

- Following the initial difficulties of political and economic transition towards a market economy, the Polish city managed to consolidate the strong position it holds today.
- In 2010, the Silesian Foundation for Support of Enterprises had 355 trainees and consulted 34 people. Moreover, approximately 50% of those found a job (Fayman et al., 2011).
- As of 2011, the training project organized by the LDA led to the creation of 22 new enterprises.
- The percentage of people employed by SMEs in Gliwice in 2011 was almost 40%, compared to some 29% at the national level in Poland. Long-term employment results still need to be assessed.
- The integration of all local actors (the municipality, its agencies (LDA, NGO center), academic institutions, R&D and business sectors) was found to be essential in the process.

***

3.2.3 Innovation

The ability to create new ideas, products and services is very much associated with economic success and economic development. Cities create smart ecosystems where skilled people are connected to each other, enabling innovation, knowledge, research, ideas and creativity to flourish and accelerate. In recent decades, **as economies have become more knowledge-intense, the role of cities and the importance of innovation has also increased**. In fact, innovation is key for achieving long-term sustainable growth. Cities need to embrace new technologies and innovations that will enable them to do more with less, and to adapt to future challenges and opportunities.

Local governments need to work together with other stakeholders to promote a culture of innovation and entrepreneurship by expanding R&D expenditure, since innovations are often the result of research and development; incentivizing university-industry linkages, as well as university-industry-government innovation models; supporting science, technology and innovation-related education and training programs; and by attracting talent and human capital. This support is especially important in developing countries, where the lack of innovation capacity presents an important barrier to the adoption and adaptation of new technologies and innovative business models (New Climate Economy, 2014).

Innovation Districts

One of the most recent trends in cities around the world for encouraging innovation, easing the exchange of ideas, and promoting entrepreneurial culture is the creation of **Innovation Districts**. Innovation districts are the result of the increasing importance of knowledge-based economies and are based on the notion that proximity and density are key contributors to business productivity.

Innovation districts can be defined as "geographic areas where leading-edge anchor institutions and companies cluster and connect with start-ups, business incubators, and accelerators." (Katz and Wagner, 2014). Innovation districts attract a mix of firms from different sectors, such as high-tech, digital, creative and research, among others. They foster collaboration among firms, allowing talent and new ideas to grow, and creating new employment. Many cities and metropolitan areas around the world are developing these innovation districts. Some examples are: Barcelona's 22@ innovation district, London's Tech City, Pittsburgh's Ecoinnovation District and Stockholm's innovation district, among many others.

Chapter 3: Cities as Enablers of Sustainable Economic Prosperity

New business models

New applied technologies and innovations

BEST PRACTICE: BOSTON
— Innovation District

Boston is the capital and largest city in the state of Massachusetts (USA), and one of the oldest cities in the United States. With a population of some 656,000 inhabitants (2014) in approximately 125 km², the city of Boston is the center of a larger area called Greater Boston, which is home to roughly 4.5 million people. The city is an economic hub and an important center of innovation in the US. In 2014, Boston's per capita income was of US$34,770, with a median household income of US$55,448 (Boston Redevelopment Authority, 2016).

Boston, USA

Source: Pixabay, CC0.

Context

- In the 1950s, after the industrial peak at the beginning of the 20th century, Boston was facing important economic troubles. As a result, Boston lost 30% of its residents over the next 30 years.

- However, from the 1960s to the 1990s, the city recovered, transforming itself into an innovation hub, with an important concentration of higher education institutions, research and manufacturing capabilities and venture capital firms by the beginning of the 21st century.

- The city and metropolitan areas are home to some of the most well-known universities and academic institutions, such as MIT, Harvard, Boston University, Tufts University and Babson College.

Actions

- In January 2010, Boston's Mayor Thomas Menino launched the Boston Innovation District, a City of Boston initiative that has the aim of helping economic recovery after the crisis and transforming the South Boston Waterfront into an urban environment that fosters innovation, collaboration and entrepreneurship.

- This project was the result of Mayor Menino's vision to redevelop the Seaport District into the "Innovation District." The vision has four main features: industry-agnostic (i.e. open to industries of every kind); clusters of innovative entrepreneurs; experimental framework; and the city as a host of universities and research firms (Rodriguez, Congdon and Ampelas, 2015).

- The project has three core objectives: urban lab, sustainable leadership and shared innovation. Moreover, the Boston I/D also aims to promote collaboration among innovative people and provide public space to foster innovative ecosystems.

- The Boston Innovation District, also known as the South Boston Waterfront or the Seaport District, spans approximately 1,000 acres of underdeveloped land and includes five sub-districts: Fort Point, Seaport, Port, Convention Center and 100-Acres.

- The area is used for different activities, from tech meetups, to co-working spaces, to start-up launches, to exhibitions and events.

- Most of the land is privately held, so there is no financial burden for the City Council in this regard. The Mayor's team focused on identifying emerging companies looking for working spaces that could be recruited to the District (Rodriguez et al., 2015).

- The Innovation District sought to become an area for entrepreneurs not only to work, but also to live and socialize, with affordable and suitable housing options.

Outcomes

- Despite being a small city, Boston has become one of the world's best well-known academic centers, an international hub of innovation, and a reference for talent and innovation attraction.

- The Innovation District area has grown rapidly and still more square feet are planned to be developed in the district. The growth is spread across a diverse range of companies in different sectors and at different scales, contributing to the city's reputation for tech-driven entrepreneurship.

- As of the beginning of 2015, Boston had the highest concentration of startup companies in the US and the city was situated among the top destinations for venture capital investments, only after the San Francisco Bay Area.

- Since 2010, and as of summer 2015, more than 200 startups have been established in the area, creating over 5,000 new jobs.

- According to the Boston's Innovation District webpage, technology companies have contributed 30% of this new job growth; creative industries - including design and advertising - have contributed 21% of new jobs; while green-tech and life science have provided 16% of new jobs (Innovation District, 2015).

- Regarding the new companies, 11% are in the education and non-profit sectors, 40% are sharing space in co-working spaces and incubators, and 25% are small-scale companies, with 10 employees or fewer.

- 40% of the new companies share space in co-working spaces and incubators. Moreover, many more companies have announced plans to join the Innovation District community, adding more jobs to the neighborhood.

- Some of the Business Accelerators and City Labs that have been established in the area are: MassChallenge, Babson Boston, Fraunhofer Center for Sustainability Energy Systems, and MIT Senseable City Lab. MassChallenge, in particular, is one of the most important entities in the city, since it is the largest accelerator of start-ups in the world with headquarters in Boston. From 2009 to 2015, MassChallenge supported 617 start-ups from around the world, providing advice for consolidation, financing and expansion of business projects.

- Problems have also emerged in the neighborhood, since rents have

Institute of Contemporary Art in South Boston

Source: Pixabay, CC0.

experienced increases and some original area tenants had to relocate to other areas of the city.

- Important cross-sectorial partnerships have been forged. In 2014, the new Mayor of Boston, Martin Walsh, created the *Neighborhood Innovation District Committee,* which includes more than 25 members from all sectors and has the goal of identifying best practices for developing neighborhood innovation districts and designing a pilot for a neighborhood-based innovation district (Rodriguez et al., 2015).

- Boston hold the 4th position in the 2thinknow *Innovation Cities Index 2015* (2thinknow, 2015).

Incubators and Accelerators

Cities have become laboratories for innovation and change. Incubators, accelerators and city labs have become other important tools for innovation and new business models, reshaping the tech industry and nurturing a city's start-up scene. These tools provide support for early-stage ventures and help an entire generation of start-ups and young companies to grow, prosper and increase the likelihood of commercial success.

Incubators "incubate" ideas with the objective of creating a company or a business model, while **accelerators help "accelerate" the growth of an existing young company**. Start-ups that participate in incubators are often more focused on innovation, and start-ups in accelerators are usually on the edge of launching revenue-generating activities. New trends and forms of start-up instruments are co-working spaces, creative labs and Fab Labs.

Chapter 3: Cities as Enablers of Sustainable Economic Prosperity

> New business models

> Policies, legislation and regulations

BEST PRACTICE: BERLIN
– A Thriving Start-Up Scene

Berlin is the capital and largest city of Germany, and one city-state among 16 German federal states. With a population of some 3.4 million inhabitants (2014) in an area of 891.7 km², Berlin is a very cosmopolitan city with a total of 16.5% of Berlin's population born outside of Germany, in many different nations (IHK and HWK, 2015). The city is well known as a cultural and economic center, as well as an important tourist attraction. In 2015 alone, the German capital had nearly 12 million visitors. Additionally in 2013, the gross domestic product per capita was of €31,504 and the disposable income per resident of a little bit above of €17,000 (IHK and HWK, 2015).

Berlin, Germany

Source: Pixabay, CC0.

Context

- Berlin was divided after World War II and has been united again since Germany's reunification in 1990. Since then, Berlin's economy has remained in transformation.

- The city's economy is not as industrial as other German cities, with some 80% of the Berlin's economy based on the service sector and high-tech firms. Berlin has a broader and more diverse creative sector, and an extensive and vibrant cultural scene.

- The German capital has also a relatively low cost of living. Rental costs in the city are much cheaper than in other German cities such as Munich, Frankfurt, Stuttgart, Hamburg or Cologne.

Actions

- Because of these factors, Berlin has become a new hub for startups, attracting thousands of local and foreign innovative entrepreneurs and creative minds.

- To promote and encourage this, the city of Berlin provides an extensive landing support for businesses that want to start out, operate and expand in the city, allowing them to try out the German capital for a few months at minimal cost. For instance, its Business Welcome Package, operated by the Berlin Partner for Business and Technology, of just approx. €4,500 for a period of 3 months, provides entrepreneurs with an office, an apartment and a customized initial consultancy on marketing, taxation and finance (Gibson, Robinson, and Cain, 2015).

- Additionally, by creating the business entity form 'Unternehmergesellschaft' (UG), the disadvantages of the "limited" form were eliminated, allowing the setup of a new business to occur much faster (Holtschke, 2016).

- In the last few years, many accelerators and incubators have also popped up all over the city, some of them inside universities. A few of the most well-known incubators and accelerators in Berlin are: MCube Incubator, the Project Flying Elephant, Startup Bootcamp, YouIsNow, Axel Springer Plug and Play, Berlin Startup Academy, hub:raum of Deutsche Telekom and Humboldt Venture Zone of the HU university. Some of these incubators provide good conditions for entrepreneurs, such as the hub:raum's incubator program in Berlin, which offers comprehensive seed financing package for the first 6 to 12 months, for 10 to 15% equity in exchange.

- The city also boasts numerous co-working spaces, such as Betahaus, Ahoy Berlin, Cluboffice, etc., which has led to increased sharing of knowledge and best practices among entrepreneurs.

- The city government has also worked to improve the city's IT infrastructures to facilitate business, and there is a plan to provide a free general WiFi network throughout the city, which will substantially help small local IT companies (Holtschke, 2016).

- With a growth in accelerators, incubators, and other initiatives from big companies and the government, Berlin has proven to be an important start-up capital in Europe.

Outcomes

- As a result of those initiatives, the ICT, media and creative industries cluster in the Berlin-Brandenburg area is one of the most important ones, with 46,920 companies (2011), 238,287 employees (2012) and 28.3 billion euros of revenues (2011) (IHK and HWK, 2015).

- The entrepreneurial and start-up sector is experiencing incredible growth. In 2010, there were roughly 42,700 registered start-ups in Berlin, which translates to 124 start-ups for every 10,000 inhabitants – ranking first among all the federal states in Germany (BWK GmbH, 2011).

- Many startups have emerged because of all these factors over the past couple of years. Some of Berlin's most notable start-ups that have already succeeded in the city are Zalando, ResearchGate, 6Wunderkinder, Soundcloud and Wooga. According to a study by McKinsey, Berlin startups will have generated up to 100,000 jobs by 2020 (McKinsey Berlin, 2013).

- According to the 2015 Startup Ecosystem Report, Berlin ranks 9th in the global ranking, and ranks the second European city, just after London (Hermann et l., 2015).

- Economic growth and employment is growing in Berlin. In 2015 alone, 41,400 new enterprises were set up and 38,000 new jobs were created (IHK and HWK, 2015). However, the unemployment rate continues to be high in comparison to the rest of Germany, at 11%.

- Berlin is now being called an incubator for innovation, the European start-up hub, and even the "European Silicon Valley."

***

3.2.4 Economic Clusters

City governments can foster competitiveness and productivity in their communities in many different ways. One possible approach is to encourage and promote urban agglomeration economies, as mentioned in Section 2. Although agglomeration is something that local governments cannot create through policy, they can promote or stimulate it through different actions and initiatives. One of the most well-known initiatives to promote agglomeration is the "**cluster approach.**"

Michael Porter defines clusters as "geographic concentrations of interconnected companies, specialized suppliers, service providers, firms in related industries, and associated institutions (e.g., universities, standards agencies, trade associations) in a particular field, linked by commonalities and complementarities." (Porter, 2000). More than single industries, clusters encompass a range of linked industries and other entities, representing critical masses of skilled labor, information, relationships, and infrastructures in that field, which raises the competitive advantage of a particular location.

Clusters have long been recognized as key drivers of economic growth and competitiveness in nations, regions and cities around the world. Clusters are usually positively correlated with job growth, productivity, wages and new business formation. Clusters promote both competition and cooperation, increase productivity and efficiency, stimulate and enable innovation, allow job growth and facilitate new business formation (Porter, 1998). They have the potential to aggregate more than the sum of their parts, due to various spillovers. In the case of cities, clusters have become central to bringing key agglomeration benefits to local economies.

Many different factors can drive cluster formation and cluster development: natural resources, geographical location, business environment conditions, existing clusters, local business, investment by firms, market dynamics, technological trends, government policies to strength clusters, etc. In general, two types of clusters or industrial agglomerations can take place: spontaneous formations and planned complexes. The spontaneous cluster originates from natural processes, while planned clusters are created as the product of local or national development policies implemented by local governments.

Chapter 3: Cities as Enablers of Sustainable Economic Prosperity

Although every cluster evolves through a different process and has its own idiosyncrasy, and therefore cannot be replicated, different examples suggest that intervention by local governments can be productive in some cases. This intervention can range from high-impact direct intervention to a low-term impact indirect intervention. In the case of the former, city managers can directly invest in the cluster creation or create dedicated city services for it. In the latter, mayors can simple facilitate collaboration with local business and academia, and within the cluster; collaborate with national governments to leverage specific programs or initiatives; or improve the cluster-specific business environment.

City planners and administrations developing cluster policies in a specific city must have a good knowledge of the city's own endowments and resources, its strengths and weaknesses, know who the different actors and stakeholders involved are and how they can or cannot collaborate. Ideally, **a bottom-up approach should be the strategic line to develop to achieve long-term competitiveness**. City managers should identify existing local activities with potential, and support and built upon them.

> Policies, legislation and regulations

> New applied technologies and innovations

BEST PRACTICE: JERUSALEM
— BioJerusalem Cluster

Jerusalem is one of the oldest cities in the world. Both Israel and Palestine claim it as a capital, but Israel maintains its primary governmental institutions there. Jerusalem has a population of more than 800,000 residents, with some 65% being Jews and non-Arabs and 35% being Arabs. The city has an area of 125 km² and the metropolitan area covers 652 km². Currently, Jerusalem remains a core issue in the Israeli-Palestinian conflict.

Context

- In early 2000s, poverty was one of the greatest economic challenges of the local government. Jerusalem had low workforce participation, lower salaries compared to the national average and 32.3% of the population was living under the poverty line (NYC Global Partners, 2010).

Jerusalem

Source: Pixabay, CC0.

- Jerusalem had highly skilled human capital and the city is home to world class institutions and universities. However, the city had difficulties retaining university graduates and being able to translate its advantages into sustainable economic growth for the city.

- There were few large national or international firms.

- There were some emerging clusters with linkages among them, but they lacked related and supporting industries.

- The physical infrastructure in the city is satisfactory.

Actions

- A series of independent studies were conducted between the years 2002-2005 and several BioMedical clusters were identified as economic drivers for Jerusalem, based on existing biomedical infrastructure and potential for growth.

- With the aim of boosting Jerusalem's economic growth and development and strengthening the local life science industry, Jerusalem's authorities decided to capitalize on the abovementioned valuable assets and turn Jerusalem into the heart of Israel's biomedical industry.

- In 2006, the Jerusalem Development Authority (JDA) launched the BioJerusalem initiative to foster the growth of the biomedical sector in the city. BioJerusalem was created to develop a leading cluster of sustainable life science enterprises by fostering solid investments, grounded in cutting-edge innovation.

- A steering committee, which included all major stakeholders in the Jerusalem BioMedical cluster, was created to guarantee optimal planning and implementation.

- JDA allocated an initial 10 million NIS through the BioJerusalem initiative, supplemented by additional funds of up to 100 million NIS (some $20 million USD) over the next five years of the program until 2012 (BioJerusalem, 2007, 2009).

- Companies with a presence in the city also benefit from a series of municipal initiatives offered by JDA, such as financial incentives (e.g. government grant of up to 20% of tangible fixed assets; significant corporate tax reduction down to 9%; and employment grants of up to 20% of salaries for 4 years for companies employing at least 15 high-wage employees (BioJerusalem, 2015)).

- Some of the main strategic goals of BioJerusalem cluster are: to increase awareness and visibility of the city's technology assets in the biomedical fields; attract companies and investments and retain the existing companies; develop cutting-edge R&D infrastructure; foster connections in the sector; and encourage and facilitate the creation of new companies.

Outcomes

- As a result of BioJerusalem, BioMedical cluster has become an economic driver for the city.

- Currently, Jerusalem hosts some of the leading research institutes in Israel, such as Hebrew University and Hadassah and Shaare Zedek Hospitals. Moreover, a unique biomedical park has been built.

- Over 50% of Israel's clinical research is conducted in Jerusalem.

- In 2007, there were 90 life science companies in Jerusalem. In 2009, this had experienced a growth of 20%. Today, there are more than 130 life science companies in the city, from entrepreneurial start-ups to more established biotech medical devices and pharmaceutical companies (BioJerusalem, 2007, 2009; BioJerusalem, 2015).

- The number of people employed by Jerusalem's life sciences companies has risen from 2,300 people before the BioJerusalem cluster initiative to 3,500 people today. This represents over 50% growth in the number of life science employees, which denotes a significant proportion of the total workforce employed in technology-based industries in the city (Biojerusalem, 2015).

Chapter 3: Cities as Enablers of Sustainable Economic Prosperity

Policies, legislation and regulations

New applied technologies and innovations

BEST PRACTICE: GUADALAJARA
— Mexico's Silicon Valley

Guadalajara is the capital and the largest city of the state of Jalisco and one of the most important metropolitan areas and economic hubs in Mexico. The city of Guadalajara is home to some 1.5 million people, while the metropolitan area hosts more than 4 million people, making it the second most populous metropolitan area in Mexico. Since colonial times, the city has been the main commercial and economic hub in Western Central Mexico. With a GDP of some $39 million, the Guadalajara Metropolitan area is the second largest economy of Mexico and one of the most developed economies in the country. The state of Jalisco in 2009 had a GDP per capita of US$6,237 (Arber, Chick, DeLoyola, Mogollon, and Novick, 2009). The city's economy is based on two main sectors: commerce/tourism and industry.

Guadalajara, Mexico

Source: Pixabay, CC0.

Context

- The city owns a strategic location: it is situated on both Mexico's Pacific Trade corridor and NAFTA corridor, which creates important advantages for the city's economy (Palacios, 2005).

- Since the 1960s, a process of developing electronic manufacturing and ICT clusters began. By the 1980s, many high technology companies were already based in Guadalajara. In the late 1990s, Guadalajara's emerging electronics cluster continued to grow and diversify, experiencing the greatest boom in the second half of the 1990s.

- Guadalajara is home to over 40 universities.

Actions

- During the 1990s, when the greatest IT cluster boom took place, the state government of Jalisco implemented a number of policies aimed at promoting the electronics industry, which proved to be very effective.

- When defining and implementing the cluster development policies, close Public-Private partnership occurred between the government and the private companies operating in the region, as well as with local industry associations, such as the American Chamber of Commerce (AmCham) and the Electronics, Telecommunications and Informatics Industry National Chamber (CANETI) and Jalisco Industrial Chamber Council (CCIJ) (Palacios, 2005).

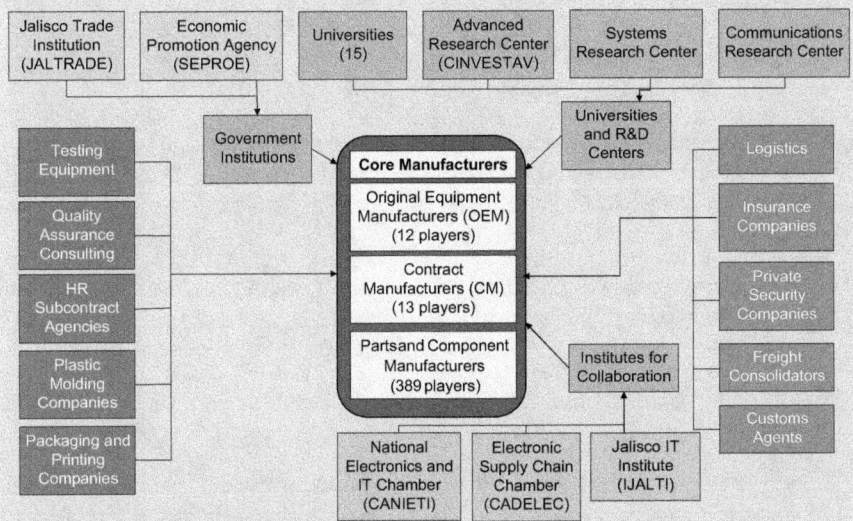

Guadalajara IT Cluster Map

Source: Own elaboration based on Arber et al. (2009).

- To promote development of the sector, several governmental institutions were established. For instance, in 1994 the Jalisco State Economic Promotion Council (CEPE) was created to promote investment, expand physical infrastructure and support employee technical training. In 2004, the Jalisco State Economic Council for Development and Competitiveness was established with representatives of the private, public and academic sectors to formulate recommendations for promoting sustainable development and competitiveness.

- Some regulations and programs regarding industrial promotion, taxation, telecommunication, among other areas have been introduced.

Outcomes

- Guadalajara has managed to take advantage of its strengths, such as its location and own industry, create a favorable business environment for both domestic and foreign companies and become the main center of high-tech industries in Mexico. It is now known as the "Mexican Silicon Valley."

- By 2010, 12 original equipment manufacturers (OEMs), more than 700 electronic manufacturing companies and several design centers were established in Guadalajara (WEF, 2014)

- Today Guadalajara has the highest concentration of IT-electronics talent and companies in Mexico, and it ranks very high in Latin America. LG, Samsung, Sony, Siemens, IBM, HP, Oracle, Dell, Intel, Solectrom, among many others, have operations in Guadalajara (Webber, 2015; WEF, 2014).

- By 2010, these IT and electronic industries exported over $17 billion worth of goods (almost 60% of exports), the highest figure in this sector in Mexico (Arber et al., 2009; WEF, 2014)

- The dense institutional framework and policy environment built in the Jalisco state, and particularly in Guadalajara and surroundings, has been critical for supporting investors who set up new ventures. Close public-private partnership and cooperation have also proven to be key in the process.

- In 2009, the sector employed 78,500 people, experiencing a 10.4% increase from 2004 to 2009 (Arber et al., 2009).

- The city has developed extensive business networks within an entrepreneurial culture, hosting meetings such as "iTuesdays and Hackers & Founders," bringing innovative ideas into contact with potential investors (Webber, 2015).

- The city's clusters have had spillover effects on the region. The state of Jalisco has 24% of the software development market, 34% of the high-tech industry and 56% of the electronic industry in Mexico (WEF, 2014).

- Taking advantage of the already-developed high-tech clusters, in 2012 Guadalajara was selected as *"Ciudad Creativa Digital",* a project that aims to become the largest hub for the digital media industry in Latin America. The *"Ciudad Creativa Digital"* project is an example of a clear trend towards diversification and how developing a cluster can have different spillover effects.

Special Economic Zones (SEZ)

Economic clusters are abundant in a variety of forms: technology clusters (as seen before), special economic zones, industrial zones, free zones, etc. Here we will focus on Special Economic Zones (SEZ). There is no single definition of Special Economic Zone (SEZ), but it usually refers to a geographical delimited area that offers incentives and benefits for investors, such as tax and tariff relief or other custom benefits. It includes a wide range of formulas such as free trade zones, export-processing zones, industrial parks, economic and technology development zones, high-tech zones, science and innovation parks, free ports, enterprise zones and others (Zeng, 2015). **The main objective of SEZ is to attract foreign direct investment (FDI) and to create employment.**

The number of SEZ has risen sharply since the 1980s. However, mixed economic results have been observed. For instance, China and other East Asia "tigers" have been very successful, but regions in sub-Saharan Africa have not.

BOX 2. Shenzhen Special Economic Zone

Shenzhen is a Chinese port city located north of the Hong Kong Administration Region. Shenzhen SEZ is one of the most well-known cases of success: the city has transformed from a small fishing village to a cosmopolitan city and a huge manufacturing center of some 10 million people. Shenzhen was one of the fastest-growing cities in the world during the 1990s and the 2000s, and is now a major financial center and home to numerous high-tech company HQs.

In 1980, the Chinese government decided to establish the first SEZ of the country in Shenzhen. It has served as an "experiment" and "learning field" for the country for introducing institutional reforms and opening up to the world. Since its establishment, city managers have implemented a series of important regulatory reforms, such as "the selling out of state-land-use rights, the stock-exchange pilot, the personnel system reform, and the minimizing of administrative approval procedure" (Zeng, 2010). Shenzhen experienced a progressive industrialization process, working from low-value products to higher-tech products. Its industrial growth has been very important for its economic development.

The city also developed an open export-oriented economy and implemented policies to attract investment (foreign and domestic). Both foreign-trade and attraction of FDI have been key in the city's success. The city also introduced initiatives to attract talented people. Shenzhen's government also encouraged technological innovations and the growth of high-tech industries to improve and advance the city's economy in more added-value industries.

As a result of all of these policy reforms, Shenzhen is now one of China's most important manufacturing bases, a high-tech research and development center, and one of the most productive cities in the country, with an income per capita of RMB 89,814 in 2008 (Zeng, 2010). Additionally, it managed to create jobs and raise people's incomes. After Shenzhen's SEZ experience, the Chinese government established seven other special economic zones in the country. Shenzhen is a good example of technological SEZ progress and how to promote innovation in the local economy.

Shenzhen, China

Source: Pixabay, CCO.

***

3.3 Facilitating the Transformation into New Urban Economies

In recent years, the economies of cities have entered a process of rapid change due to economic globalization, new technologies, an intensive use of ICTs, an increased competition between territories, the relocation or cessation of many activities of the past (especially industrial activities), the rise of the knowledge economy, among many other factors. These **current dynamics of change are transforming urban economic realities into a new and exceptional system**, posing new and old challenges to local governments, while offering new opportunities in different sectors.

These new opportunities are creating the so-called "new urban economies," which are the result of some of the leverages of change of our model, mentioned at the beginning of Section 3. For instance, rapid technological change and innovations are giving rise to a new *digital economy*. Additionally, changes in people's preferences and behaviors are allowing the development of more sustainable ways of producing, such as the *circular economy* or the *green economy,* and new ways of consuming, such as the *sharing economy*. In this section, we will present some of these new urban economies, as well as a few examples of different initiatives or study cases about them.

Although it is true that local governments cannot develop new economies by themselves, they can facilitate new urban economies with the capacity to transform threats and weaknesses of the new global economic scenario into local opportunities and strengths for both the city and its inhabitants.

3.3.1 Digital Economy and the Economy of Data

The use of new technologies and ICTs are disrupting today's urban economies, changing how people, firms and governments work and interact; opening up new business; creating new jobs; and affecting the way cities function. In particular, digitalization and the diffusion and ubiquity of the internet are changing entire industries, profoundly impacting many sectors of the economy and giving rise to new-digital related business in the so-called *digital economy*. New digital technology innovations such as smartphones, mobile-based sensing, the internet-of-things (IoT), Big Data, data analytics, social media, and others are fueling this trend.

Industries such as transportation, healthcare, media, retail, banking and manufacturing are undergoing important transformations. Online banking, digital tax payments, online education, e-shopping, and even the implementation of IoT-based healthcare services are the result of the impressive spread and ubiquitous nature of new digital technologies.

In general terms, the adoption of new digital technology businesses can enhance efficiency, reduce costs and ease the relations between customers and business partners. This, in turn, fuels growth, innovation and productivity. It also offers a more diversified economy. However, it often forces the reorganization of traditional business and affects labor demands. For instance, in the case of the retail industry, the internet offers a huge sales outlet with the possibility of accessing wider markets and potential growth through online shopping. But then again, it also affects traditional retail business models and workers in those sectors. Therefore, it is important to find a way to adapt to these transformations in a balanced and sustainable manner.

Additionally, the digitalization of public services and other e-government initiatives can change how citizens deal and interact with the administration and can help city governments demonstrate transparency, build trust with citizens, obtain efficiency gains for the public administration, save taxpayers money and deliver better services for citizens.[8]

---

[8] All these issues are going to be studied in the volumes *Cities and Governance* and *Cities and Public Management*.

Although we are going to study the issues of new applied technologies such as big data and IoT in detail in the book volume *Cities and Technology*, it is worth mentioning here since city data is an important disruptive force in new urban economies, creating new business models, transforming many economic sectors, enabling new services and generating employment.

Big Data

One of the most profound impacts of digitalization can be seen in "big data." **Big data refers to large amounts of data that is now more available thanks to digitalization**. Big data covers many different sectors and industries, including transportation, energy and healthcare. It can create value through various means, from business processes optimization to enhancing customer experiences.

A data-driven economy can foster research and innovation, create more business opportunities and increase availability of knowledge and capital. In the case of cities, big data and data-driven innovation have become central to local economic development and for managing public services. The availability of large amounts of data can help solve contemporary urban challenges, as exhibited in the different volumes of this series. In fact, **cities are the ultimate enabler of the data economy**. For instance, we have seen that big data can help manage and regulate traffic, achieve energy savings thanks to smart energy grids and manage parking problems.[9]

---

[9] All these issues are developed in depth in the respective book volumes or in the upcoming book *Cities and Technology*.

BOX 3. Enerbyte – Data and Digital Economy for Energy Efficiency

The mobile applications market is probably one of the most rapidly growing data-economy sectors. The European App Economy report 2016, which examines the app market within the European Union, estimates that **the app economy contributed almost 2 million jobs in the EU in 2015** (Wilcox and Voskoglou, 2015).

One good example of applying new technologies to generate valuable data for creating new business opportunities is the app **enerbyte**. At the same time, it achieves energy efficiency goals, improves the environment and produces individual and social benefits. The app is a Virtual Energy Advisor that aims to help users save energy and reduce energy usage by changing citizens' behavior. The app also enhances collaboration with the city community by sharing and combining savings with other members from a community (Enerbyte, 2016). The company won the 1st prize at the Barcelona Smart City App Hack in 2015 and it was also a finalist for other awards.

Enerbyte has collaborated in a number of projects in different cities in Spain. One example is the "Rubi Brilla" project with the city council of Rubi, a municipality in the Province of Barcelona. The project seeks to make energy efficiency improvements through behavioral change. By using the program Personal Energy, citizens using it to control their consumption saved on average 23% more energy than users from the community that didn't use the platform.

Open Data

Thanks to digitalization, the "sharing of information" is now easier than ever before. The digital revolution has allowed city governments to make city data freely and publicly available to everyone for use. Such initiatives are known as **Open Data initiatives**. Open data can be defined as "data that can be freely used, re-used and redistributed by anyone - subject only, at most, to the requirement to attribute and share-alike" (Open Data Handbook, 2012). These initiatives seek to facilitate access to information for citizens, businesses and organizations and to impact different sectors or areas.

First, open data improves government by ensuring **governments' transparency and accountability**. Second, it **creates economic opportunities** by fostering business innovation and job creation. By opening data, local governments can help entrepreneurs to develop and establish new business and services, enable developers to create innovative applications and accelerate overall economic growth. Third, it **empowers citizens** to make more informed decisions. And lastly, open data can also **help solve public problems**, by keeping citizens informed about heath and natural disaster concerns (Verhulst and Young, 2016). In this book, we are going to focus on the second potential impact of opening data, i.e. how open data can help create business opportunities.

According to a 2013 McKinsey report, open data and shared data initiatives in seven sectors alone (education, transport, consumer products, electricity, oil and gas, healthcare and consumer finance) could help create globally more than $3 trillion a year in additional value (Manyika et al., 2013). They also have the potential to create new employment opportunities and add social value to communities. In the case of the European Union, it is estimated that the reuse of data will create a market of some €55 billion and create around 75,000 direct open data jobs in 2016 alone, while providing accumulated public savings of around €1.7 billion in 2020 for the EU (European Union, 2015). Open data initiatives also face several challenges, such as technological problems and concerns regarding privacy and data protection. These issues will need to be addressed soon in order to unleash its full potential.

> New applied technologies and innovations

> Policies, legislation and regulations

BEST PRACTICE: NEW YORK
— NYC Business Atlas to Create Business Opportunities

New York is the most populous city in the United States and one of the most important economic, financial, cultural and political centers of the world. It has around 8.5 million inhabitants in an area of 1,214 km² with an urban density of 10,756/km². NYC is a global hub of business and commerce, and the world's premier financial center. In 2012, the New York City Metropolitan Area generated a gross metropolitan product (GMP) of over US$1.33 trillion. Moreover, in 2013, the metropolitan area of NY-NJ-PA had a GDP per capita of US$69,074.

New York, USA

Source: Pixabay, CC0.

Context

- Lack of good quality information about economic conditions in neighborhoods was a common problem for small entrepreneurs and small business in the city of New York.

- In 2013, the City of New York created the Mayor's Office of Data Analytics (MODA) to take advantage and make use of the large amounts of data that the city was generating. MODA works on crime prevention, disaster response, improving public services, economic development and created NYC's Open Data portal (https://nycopendata.socrata.com/) (Young, Sangokoya, and Verhulst, 2016).

Actions

- In the same year, 2013, the recently created MODA department, together with the NYC Department of Information Technology & Telecommunications and the Department of Small Business Services created the "NYC Business Atlas." The NYC Business Atlas is an interactive map aimed at supporting small local business development and economic growth by providing an easy-to-use tool with good analytics information.
- The NYC Business Atlas was created to overcome a lack of information problem by creating a public tool that provides small retail entrepreneurs and businesses access to high-quality information about the economic conditions of the neighborhoods in which they operate.
- The NYC Business Atlas gathers a diversity of data, including business-filing data from the Department of Consumer Affairs, sales tax data from the Department of Finance, demographic data from the census, and traffic data from Placemeter, a New York City startup focusing on real-time traffic information (Young et al., 2016).
- With this data, entrepreneurs and small business owners can access information including population distribution, new businesses activity, median household income, and taxable sales revenue, among others. This information can help them decide where to establish their new storefronts or where to expand.
- The city government also trains workers in its business solutions centers to teach small business owners how to use the tool (Furman, 2013).

NYC Business Atlas

Source: https://maps.nyc.gov/businessatlas

Outcomes

- The main beneficiaries of the initiative have been small business owners, which usually lack the resources to access useful information. The information contained on the Business Atlas has helped them make better-informed decisions when looking for suitable (or unsuitable) neighborhoods in which to operate.

- However, the governments' challenge now is to be able to reach more people and make them aware of the availability of this information (Young et al., 2016).

- The Business Atlas and MODA's work have stimulated the development of other similar open data projects. In fact, New York is now considered a leader in open data initiatives worldwide.

- The NYC Business Atlas is a good example of how a Mayor's Office can go beyond just "opening" raw data by providing analysis of the data that can help drive economic growth and overcome problems related to a lack of information faced by small businesses and entrepreneurs.

- It is also a good example of how public-private collaborations in terms of data can help economic growth and develop new business opportunities.

Internet-of-Things

Another area that is also experiencing striking growth and that represents the next step towards the digitalization of our economy is the so-called **Internet-of-Things** (IoT). IoT refers to the digital interconnection of physical devices or objects by means of the internet, which enables these objects to collect and exchange data.

IoT offers significant opportunities to cities and businesses alike by creating a more direct integration of the physical world into computer-based systems, improving efficiency and providing economic benefits. In the case of cities, IoT brings together people, processes, data and things to make connections more relevant and valuable to help city leaders manage and deliver urban services more efficiently. For instance, IoT can allow city mangers to better manage traffic flows, to provide enhanced waste and water systems, or to improve building management or healthcare systems.

All in all, city governments should take advantage of all the benefits that new technologies, digitalization and big data offer to both cities and local businesses to foster local sustainable economic development and facilitate business, economic prosperity and a better quality of life. Adapting to digital technologies is critical to thrive and survive in today's modern economy. Cities and local governments should have a leading role in enabling and facilitating this transformation into new urban economies.

BOX 4. IoT Healthcare Platform in Daegu City (South Korea)

The Government of Korea initiated in 2015 an IoT-based healthcare services project to promote digital economy, respond to healthcare challenges posed by the world's ageing population, foster economic growth and facilitate job creation. The Daegu Consortium, a PPP formed by the Daegu Metropolitan City and private sector partners (including big companies such as KT Corporation and Samsung Electronics, but also SMEs, and collaborative networks such as Daegu Technopark), was chosen by the Korean Government, who also joined the consortium. The association receives KRW5.2 billion (some US$4.5 million) in funding for the first phase of the project. The total cost of the project, which lasts 3 years, is expected to be around KRW13 billion (Daegu, 2015).

The main objective of the project is to improve citizen's quality of life, to support business incubation schemes for SMEs with better regulatory support, and to promote competitiveness of healthcare services industry. First, in order to improve people's health, a Healthcare platform has been created, which is based on Common-IoT-Platform that uses OneM2M standards. The service provides biometric measurements and personalized exercise/diet plans to users, shares blood pressure records of patients, as well as informs the competent medical institutes. Second, from 2016 onwards, the consortium also plans to help increase public welfare by supporting and fostering more than 100 SMEs and ventures companies by 2017. In addition, the city of Daegu plans to develop a medical device and healthcare services cluster, or Healthcare Hub Center, to facilitate cooperation among the creative economy innovation centres and support the commercialization of new products by SMEs.

By making use of new technologies and digitalization, the South Korean city of Daegu aims to advance healthcare outcomes by significantly improving the quality of life of its residents and to make use of the high-tech medical industry as a new engine for local and regional economic growth.

***

3.3.2 The Green and the Circular Economy

A well-functioning economy depends, among many other things, on the environment. Although environmental issues in cities have been developed and analyzed in the book *Cities and the Environment*, it is worth briefly mentioning it here for two reasons. First, most of the contemporary environmental problems and challenges - such as rising pollution and CO_2 emissions, climate change, energy consumption or resource scarcity - are the result of economic activities. And second, because many "new economies" are trying to go green, be resource efficient and preserve the environment, which have the potential to become promising new growth drivers in cities.

Green Economy

Although there is no standardized definition for the "green economy," it can be defined as an economy that increases prosperity while maintaining the natural system that sustains human beings (European Environment Agency, 2012). In other words, an economy where resources are used efficiently, tries to emit less pollution and preserves the natural ecosystems of the planet.

As we discussed in the first volume of this series, many cities around the world have already set up many initiatives and programs to become more sustainable in general, but also to enable the economy to be more ecological. City councils, as suppliers of public intervention, are important actors when it comes to growth of the green economy, since they have the power to include sustainability as part of their economic development programs. The consumer, the producer and governments – local and national – are equally important actors in greening our economy.

The green economy can create value added in terms of new business models and GDP growth and in terms of employment creation. Green jobs – e.g. those jobs related with environmental protection and climate adaptation - are rising. For instance, in the European Union, green jobs increased from 3 to 4.2 million between 2002 and 2011 (European Commission, 2014).

BOX 5. Cleveland (Ohio): Creating green jobs through a cooperative

Cleveland is a city of almost 400,000 people in the U.S. state of Ohio. In 2008, a working group of Cleveland-based institutions (including the Cleveland Foundation, the Cleveland Clinic, University Hospitals, Case Western Reserve University) along with the City of Cleveland launched the *Evergreen Cooperatives*. Its goal was to develop ideas for environmentally friendly worker-owned businesses that could create living-wage jobs in six low-income neighborhoods of the city (Evergreen Cooperatives, 2016; NLC, 2013).

Some of the companies in the cooperative are the Evergreen Cooperative Laundry; the Evergreen Energy Solutions, a solar company developing and installing solar panels; and Green City Growers Cooperative, in the field of urban farming (Bradley, 2013).

The Cleveland initiative is a good example of an innovative, green, wealth-sharing group in one of the poorest cities in the U.S. It has been able to create employment, develop small business and get the community involved, while keeping sustainability at the core of the project.

Source: Pixabay, CC0

Circular Economy

A green economy aims to reduce the negative environmental impacts of human activities by trying to emit less pollution and use less resources. However, it does change the current linear "take-make-dispose" consumption model, which results in massive amounts of waste generated, increases the planet's scarcity problem and intensifies the use of materials and energy. In this context, **the circular economy arises as a potential solution to our current waste and resources problem by creating regenerative ways of producing, consuming and disposing products**.

The circular economy can be defined as an economy where the value of products, materials and resources is maintained in the economy for as long as possible, and the generation of waste is minimized, all with the aim of reducing resource use and emissions (European Commission, 2015a). In other words, it tries to **take a new approach to production cycles**, where instead of the "produce-consume-throw" model mentioned above, products, parts and materials are used, repaired, reused and recycled as much as possible, while minimizing the material and energy-intensity of production systems at the same time. Therefore, the circular economy is more than just recycling. It seeks to **create a new production-consumption model**, which eliminates waste by recycling and reusing it as much as possible, but also focuses on **rethinking and redesigning products and components**, creating products with the ability to reuse them inherent in the product's design.

The circular economy is the result of three important megatrends or leverages of change. First, greater urbanization, which facilitates the implementation of the circular economy. Second, advances in digital technology, which have the potential to support business development by helping to match used goods with potential reuse or remanufacture companies and markets (New Climate Economy, 2014). And third, a change in the preferences and behaviors of consumers, who are looking for new ways of consuming that are more sustainable and ecological.

Thus, new and innovative business models are already being developed, offering economic, environmental and social opportunities. According to some estimates, **the circular economy could add up to US$1 trillion to** the global economy by 2025, with 100,000 new jobs created for the next five years, while reducing greenhouse gas emissions (New Climate Economy, 2014).

Cities can be powerful catalysts of the circular economy, by incorporating circular ideas into city planning, by tackling most of the barriers that hamper the transition towards a circular economy, or by promoting businesses that rethink their waste practices. They can also encourage firms to innovate for a circular, more sustainable future.

> **BOX 6. Western Cape, South Africa - Industrial Symbioses**
>
> "Industrial symbiosis" refers to when a company's waste is another company's resource (De Groene Zaak, 2015). Building on this concept, the Western Cape Industrial Symbiosis Program (WISP) was initiated by the Western Cape Government of South Africa in 2013. Western Cape is a South African province with coasts bordering the Indian and Atlantic Oceans. The capital is the city of Cape Town.
>
> The WISP Program is funded by the WCG's Green Economy initiative, which is administered through the Department of Economic Development and Tourism (DEDAT) (De Groene Zaak, 2015). It is a free service that connects firms willing to identify business opportunities from under-used resources (materials, expertise, logistics, capacity, energy, water), in order to achieve synergies, and improve business profitability and sustainability. The program transforms the linear industrial model into an interconnected system through a web. The network is formed by different stakeholders, from businesses across diverse industries, to industry associations, and provincial and local governments.
>
> According to the WISP webpage, the synergies formed by the industrial symbiosis network had achieved the following benefits by mid-2016: 1,752 waste diversion; R5.1 million costs savings; R7.0 million additional revenue; 4,988 tons of CO_2 savings; and the creation of 14 temporary jobs and 22 permanent jobs (WISP, 2016). WISP is a good example of how to overcome the lack of information problem and high transaction costs in the circular economy through an initiative facilitated by the government. It is also a good collaborative project between different levels of government (regional and local). The project was a finalist for the 2015 Circular Economy Awards.

3.3.3 The Sharing Economy

One possible solution within the scope of the circular economy is changing the way we think of ownership and how we access products. Consumer preferences, especially younger people, are moving away from ownership, choosing the temporary access-right to a product over owning it, i.e. the idea of "access over ownership". This new trend is giving rise to the so-called sharing economy, also called "collaborative economy," "peer-to-peer economy" or "on-demand economy". Regardless of the term used, **the sharing economy refers to a socio-economic system, platform or marketplace that brings together individuals, usually by means of the internet and other information technologies, to share or exchange assets or services that otherwise would be underutilized, either for free or for monetary benefits** (Botsman, 2015; Koopman, Mitchell, and Thierer, 2014).

The value proposition of the sharing economy is the ability to facilitate connections between consumers owning underutilized goods or services and consumers in need of that resource, at the right time and with reduced transaction costs (Dervojeda et al., 2013). It also creates added value by reducing energy consumption and the need for new raw materials, as products or services can be used more often and more efficiently. Like the circular economy, the sharing economy also seeks to improve the resource scarcity problem and has sustainability at the core of its concept.

Collaborative economy initiatives have multiplied and expanded at a dizzying pace in recent years. This is partially because this type of business model or platform is not limited to one specific sector. In fact, businesses can facilitate peer-to-peer markets for almost all products and services, from transportation to accommodation, with some of the most well-known examples being Uber and Airbnb. Other areas include space, food, logistics, services, learning, freelance work, goods, money, finance, or utilities (Table 5).

Table 5: The sharing economy, some examples

Category or Sector		Companies, Start-ups or apps - Examples
Mobility and Transportation	Ridesharing	Uber, Lyft, Hailo, Grab, Sidecar, Blablacar
	Car sharing	RelayRides, Getaround, Zipcar, Autoshare, car2go
	Other vehicles sharing	Liquid, spinlister (bikes); Sailo, Boatbound (boats); Jetsharter (jets)
Space	Accommodation	Airbnb, Couchsurfing, Homeaway, VRBO
	Work space	Wework, Pivotdesk, ShareDesk, Liquidspace
	Storage	MakeSpace, Roost, Spacer, SpaceOut
Services	Personal services	Taskrabbit, Handy, DogVacay, Zaarly, fiverr
	Professional services	Upwork, Crowdspring, Hourlynerd, BidWilly
Finance	Moneylending	LendingClub, Zopa, Borrowell, Prosper
	Crowdfunding	Indigogo, Kickstarter, GoFundMe, CircleUp
	Payments	TransferWise, M-pesa
	Insurance	Friendsurance, Wesura, Inspeer, metromile
Utilities	Telecommunications	Fon, OpenGarden
	Energy	Gridmates, Vandebron
Goods	Buy and sell	Poshmark, Wallapop, eBay, Craigslist, Etsy
	Loaner products	NeighborGoods, peerby, Renttherunway, Streetbank, OpenShed
Food	Shared food	EatWith, Mealsharing, VizEat, LeftoverSwap
Learning	Peer2peer learning	P2PU, Skillshare, SharingAcademy
	Open courses	Coursera, KhanAcademy, Udemy

Source: Own elaboration.

The sharing economy offers huge economic potential for the different sectors, business and individuals involved. According to some estimates by PwC, **just five sectors of the sharing economy** – peer-to-peer accommodation, car sharing, peer-to-peer finance, music, TV and video streaming and online staffing – **could generate revenues of US$335 billion by 2025**, in comparison to the US$15 billion in revenue they generated in

2014 (Hawksworth and Vaughan, 2014). In the European Union alone, gross revenue from the sharing economy companies was estimated to be €28 billion in 2015, almost double compared to the previous year (European Commission, 2016).

Therefore, the rise of the sharing economy seems unstoppable. However, it is yet not clear exactly how and in which direction these new business models will evolve. Nor is it certain that the full growth potential of the sharing economy will be unleashed in the end. On the one hand, the sharing economy offers great economic advantages, allowing increased market access to a larger number of people, directing and allocating resources, facilitating exchanges and reducing search and information costs thanks to new technologies. It also has the potential to create new jobs for citizens. But on the other hand, **sharing economy business models have also raised concerns** about precarious work and labor conditions; impacts on established industries; safety for customers and users; minimum quality standards of the products or services; issues of fair competitive conditions and uncollected tax revenues. Moreover, there are doubts about long-term efficiency and the real "resource sharing" in these business models. Since the sharing economy affects policy at many different levels, it should be a key issue addressed by local and national governments around the world.

All in all, the topic of **weak regulation lies at the core of the debate**. In the case of cities, existing regulatory frameworks are often unprepared and outdated for these disruptive new digital start-ups and business models. However, sharing economies directly affect the functioning of cities and have the potential to transform how urban citizens access and consume services and products. Therefore, city managers and policymakers should pay special attention to the sharing and circular economies. They should try to redefine and adapt existing regulatory frameworks in a way that balances hazards and opportunities for these new business practices, promotes the innovation of the new tech startups, but protects customers, citizens and incumbent businesses. One of the main difficulties when defining new regulatory frameworks for the sharing economy is that not all the business models (see those exhibited in Table 5) function in the same way. For instance, some are just platforms connecting customers and suppliers, while others also control prices and relations. Regulating this heterogeneity is a complex matter.

Some cities, mostly in European countries, are banning or rigidly regulating these services. Others, instead, are trying to address the sharing economy with policies that accommodate or regulate the operation of sharing services in different ways. For instance, San Francisco was one of the first major cities to regulate and legalize the short-term letting company Airbnb. It was a top-priority issue for the city council, since the home-sharing company is estimated to contribute $56 million to San Francisco's local economy and support 430 jobs in the city (CITIE, 2015). However, some challenges still exist in the process of reframing regulations. Other cities have also tried temporary regulations for a trial-and-error period before a final regulation decision, such as Amsterdam with Airbnb and Portland with Uber and Lyft. Lastly, another example is the city of Singapore, which has introduced regulations to safeguard consumers when using popular taxi-booking apps such as Uber and established new regulations that encourage fair competition for business (CITIE, 2015).

While there is yet no perfect balance or regulations, city regulators need to keep trying to find a way to build a business environment with laws that keep pace with fast-changing and evolving business models. City managers should engage in consultation and collaboration with different stakeholders in each sector, with representatives of both new business models and traditional business as well as consumers and the public in general. In this way, they can create new regulatory frameworks that protect consumers and business alike. Working together is the only way that cities will be able to bring the environmental and community benefits of the sharing economy to local economies and to citizens.

> **BOX 7. Sharing Cities**
>
> Cities are the primary point where communities share: from shared infrastructures and urban services, to homes and skills. However, some cities are trying to go one step further and actively engage with opportunities in virtual commons, peer-to-peer communities and online sharing platforms to promote the sharing economy and position themselves as model cities for sharing (McLaren and Agyeman, 2016).
>
> **Seoul**
>
> The capital of South Korea was one of the first cities in the world to embrace the sharing economy. With a population of around 10 million people in 605 km², Seoul is one of the most densely populated cities in the world. Therefore, finding a solution to resource and housing scarcity and housing shortages is critical. It is also one of the most connected cities, with highly developed IT and internet services. Lastly, sharing is also something very much rooted in the culture. *Jeong* is a Korean concept used "to describe the action of giving small, gratuitous gift," and "if you don't share you will [...] have little or no *jeong*" (McLaren and Agyeman, 2015). Therefore, the city had the necessary conditions for the sharing economy to develop.
>
> To spread the Culture of Sharing, the city of Seoul initiated the "Sharing City, Seoul" project in 2012. It sought to expand digital sharing infrastructures, promote sharing economy start-ups and put public resources to better use (McLaren and Agyeman, 2015). Since then, the Seoul Metropolitan Government (SMG) has addressed various problems such as transportation, parking, residential, and environmental issues through sharing policies. SMG has developed "sharing city" infrastructure; supported 57 sharing organizations and businesses from 2013 to 2015 (and it will promote 300 businesses until 2018); launched the *Share Hub* online repository of sharing economy services; and launched campaigns for engaging citizens (Share Hub, 2015). It also plans to expand sharing actions to other areas such as food industry, insurance, tourism, etc. The city estimates the second round of sharing projects will have important economic, social and environmental benefits such as: 12 billion annual savings for citizens; 1.18 trillion saving for the city; 1,280 new jobs; and a 29,800-ton reduction of CO_2 emissions (Share Hub, 2015).

Amsterdam

The "Amsterdam Sharing City" program was founded in 2013, making the Dutch capital Europe's first sharing city. The goal of the project is to improve the digital infrastructure, promote innovation and sharing economy start-ups, and take advantage of citizens' willingness to share (some 84%).

Amsterdam has always tried to utilize the opportunities offered by the sharing economy. As mentioned before, it was one of the first cities to develop regulations for Airbnb. Additionally, the city has helped develop other sharing economy initiatives such as *Konnektid*, a skills and knowledge sharing platform, or *Peerby*, a platform enabling citizens to borrow the things they need from people in their neighborhood.

Source: Pixabay, CC0

***

3.3.4 The Creative Economy

The creative economy, also known as "cultural industries" or "creative industries," is an emerging concept based on the idea that the use of creativity, combined with advances in new technologies and ICTs, can add value to the local economy, strength existing industries, develop new ones and create jobs. Although there is no unique definition UNESCO defines it as "sectors of organized activity whose principal purpose is the production or reproduction, promotion, distribution and/or commercialization of goods, services and activities of a cultural, artistic or heritage-related nature." (UNESCO, n.d.). In other words, all economic activities where creativity, technology, culture and innovation are combined in a way that results in economic growth and employment creation.

The concept of "creative economy" was firstly popularized by John Howkins in 2001, covering different sectors from art, to culture, design, entertainment, media and innovation (Howkins, n.d.). Now, it has a wider approach covering many different sectors, from arts and craft, to books, films, paintings, festivals, music, advertising, architecture, designs, newspapers and magazines, performing arts, radio, TV, visual arts, digital animation, and video games, among others, depending on the definition used.

Today, **creative economies are among the most dynamic sectors of the global economy**. According to a report by EY Consulting and UNESCO, the cultural and creative industries generated around US$2,250 billion of revenues and 29.5 million jobs worldwide in 2013 (EY, 2015).[10] And cities are central to the global creatives' economies, since urban areas are the main places where innovation and creativity flourish. Creativity in cities is a key economic driver for local economies. Also, **creative activities often contribute significantly to youth employment**, which is important in cities to fight current high youth unemployment rates. Lastly, creativity and culture also boost cities' attractiveness, which is essential to attract human capital and talent. All in all, creative economies have an important impact on cities, both in terms of economic growth and employment creation. Thus, local governments should implement policies and initiatives that strengthen and promote creative industries to take advantage of the positives connections between creativity, innovation and competitiveness.

---

[10] The report analyzes 11 key sectors across five global regions, including visual arts, performing arts, radio, music, books, newspapers and magazines, film, television, architecture, gaming and advertising.

Policies, legislation and regulations

New business models

BEST PRACTICE: MONTREAL
– Creating a circus art city

Montreal is the second most populous city in Canada, and the largest in the region of Quebec, with some 1.6 million inhabitants in 431.50 km². The Montreal metropolitan area has some 4 million inhabitants. The city is an important center of commerce, aerospace, finance, ITC, design, culture, education and world affairs. Additionally, it is a leading city in terms of hosting international conventions (in 2015 Montreal ranked first in North America for international events, after five consecutive years in the top position).

Montreal, Canada

Source: Pixabay, CC0.

Context

- The original circus created in 18th century in London had suffered almost no modification for more than 200 years.

- By the 1980's the circus industry was changing and a new concept of circus was on the rise, with less use of animals and more theater, dance, acrobatics, lighting and music.

- In 1981, the National Circus School was created in Montreal, being the first and only school that provided circus arts training in the Western World (Berrone and Blazquez, 2013b).

- In 1984, students from the National Circus School, with the leadership of artist and visionary Guy Laliberté, organized a large-scale street show for the 450th anniversary of the discovery of Canada. He received $1 million from the government of Quebec to organize it (Berrone and Blazquez, 2013b). The event was very successful and marked the origin of the Cirque du Soleil in Canada in 1984.

- In the following years, Le Cirque du Soleil grew and expanded quickly and created many synergies and mutual dependences with the National Circus School.

Actions

- In the late 80s the mayor of Montreal Jean Doré, while preparing the economic development strategy of the city for the next five years, wondered if besides supporting traditional industries, the City Council should also consider assisting other activities, such as circus arts. This would not only have a positive economic impact on the city, but would be advantageous for its cultural implications.

- With this aim, Mr. Doré met with representatives of the two main circus institutions in Montreal, the National Circus School and Le Cirque du Soleil, in order to discuss the future of the circus industry and their role in the cultural and economic development of the region (Berrone and Blazquez, 2013a).

- In 1996, with the support of the Quebec's government, an association of companies and individuals called *En Piste* was created with the aim of helping the circus arts and implementing initiatives to generate more business opportunities for its members.

- *En Piste,* the National Circus School, and Cirque du Soleil created La TOHU, a place for "dissemination, creation, experimentation and convergence of culture, environment and community involvement."

Outcomes

- By 2007, an active community had been created around the circus cluster in Montreal, with 40 circus companies, 20 schools, several production agencies and hundreds of professional circus artists.

Cirque du Soleil, Kooza production

Source: Flickr/Derek Key

- In some Montreal districts (e.g. Villeray/Saint Michel), the circus industry accounted for 3.4% of local employment (Berrone, Blazquez, and Diego, 2013).
- Montreal is now an international leader in circus arts, with an important circus cluster.
- This is a good example of how local authorities can help facilitate collaborative action among private sector actors to achieve the most efficient collaboration and address coordination and cooperation failures in the context of the creative economy.

***

4. Concluding Remarks

Now more than ever, cities are taking a leading role in stimulating economic growth and employment in regions and countries around the world. As centers of production, innovation, creativity, trade, and connectivity, cities are unique poles of attraction for labor and capital. They are great facilitators for merging these areas in a way that creates value added, increases productivity and provides better living standards for citizens. They offer people advantageous places to live, work, play and prosper. They also provide investors optimal locations where they can launch, grow and expand their businesses. For these reasons, **cities can create better economic opportunities for all stakeholders living in them.**

However, rapid urbanization poses multiple and perilous challenges for cities and citizens, such as higher inequalities, poverty, unemployment or informality in employment, along with many other environmental and social threats (e.g. pollution, strain on the environment, resource scarcity, shortage of physical and social infrastructures, etc.). Yet **cities are particularly well suited for providing an answer to urban economic challenges.**

As we have seen in this volume, cities can be sources of job creation and income growth due to the benefits brought by agglomeration economies, face-to-face interactions and knowledge spillovers. Additionally, they host a combination of some of the most important current global megatrends, like technological breakthroughs and digitalization. As consumer behavior and preferences change and people look for different ways of producing and consuming, new dynamics are transforming urban economic realities into a new and exceptional system. **New urban economies are offering innovative opportunities for new businesses and economic activities in cities.**

Although economic development and competitiveness policies are traditionally thought of as national variables/economic units, **city managers have many instruments, policies and regulations at their disposal for influencing city economies.** In this volume, we have highlighted potential actions or initiatives that city managers can implement to enhance economic growth and competitiveness. These include improving the efficiency and quality of urban physical infrastructures and urban services; developing a favorable business environment; empowering entrepreneurship and innovation; and implementing diversification and competitiveness policies. Several best practices and case studies have been studied and they show that they can be successful if planned and managed in the right way. City managers, therefore, have a great capacity to impact a city's economic development and create employment.

While there is no single recipe for achieving economic growth, some common challenges and elements can be identified. Cities can learn and gain ideas from others when designing and implementing economic development plans. The cornerstone for city leaders is to identify and exploit the competitive advantage of their cities and adopt a strategic approach that is suitable for its own situation. First, city managers need to understand their current realities and starting points (i.e. in terms of their resource endowments, size, institutions, economic structures, business environments and levels of skills of their citizens), as well as to identify the city's main weaknesses or deficits (e.g. infrastructures or regulatory frameworks and legislations). Only after understanding these issues can city leaders carry out a strategic analysis and develop a unique set of strategies and actions that can contribute to economic development and employment creation in their cities.

City governments require collaboration with all stakeholders and on all levels of government to achieve sustainable and equitable economic growth. First, **local governments must work together with regional and national governments** to develop policies and initiatives in line with regional and national economic development plans and regional and national business legislations and regulations. Second, city managers will also require the support of the private sector to identify key challenges and create initiatives that can offer opportunities and benefits to all sectors of society. **Public-private collaboration is key to catalyze sustained economic growth and solve specific problems**. By adopting innovative collaboration frameworks, local governments can position themselves at the core of a diverse set of stakeholders and lead innovative initiatives for more inclusive and sustainable economic growth.

If local economic development is well planned and managed, and the benefits and challenges brought about by urbanization are balanced in an equitable way, urbanization can be a powerful driver of sustainable development, economic growth, prosperity and quality of life for citizens around the world.

***

5. References

2thinknow (2015). Innovation Cities Index 2015. Retrieved from http://www.innovation-cities.com/innovation-cities-index-2015-global

Arber, J., Chick, A., DeLoyola, G., Mogollon, I., and Novick, B. (2009). "Electronics Cluster in Guadalajara, Mexico: Analysis of an Unusual Cluster in a Developing Economy." (Harvard Business School, Ed.), *Microeconomics of Competitiveness.*

Berrone, P., and Blazquez, M. L. (2013a). "Creating a Cluster around a Clown: The Montreal Circus Cluster (A)". IESE, SM-1597-E (09/2013).

Berrone, P., and Blazquez, M. L. (2013b). "Creating a Cluster around a Clown: The Montreal Circus Cluster (B)". IESE, SM-1598-E (09/2013).

Berrone, P., Blazquez, M. L., and Diego, E. de (2013). "Creating a Cluster around a Clown: The Montreal Circus Cluster (C)". IESE, SM-1599-E (09/2013).

Berrone, P., Ricart, J. E., and Duch T-Figueras, A. I. (2016a). *Cities and Mobility & Transportation: Towards the Next Generation of Urban Mobility*. CreateSpace.

Berrone, P., Ricart, J.-E., and Duch T-Figueras, A. I. (2016b). *Cities and the Environment: The Challenge of Becoming Green and Sustainable*. CreateSpace.

BioJerusalem (2007). "BioJerusalem Launches Activities: Jerusalem Development Authority Allocates Initial 10 million NIS to BioJerusalem. Jerusalem: BioJerusalem." Retrieved from http://www.yissum.co.il/sites/default/files/biojerusalem_launch_final.pdf

BioJerusalem (2009). "20% Growth in the Number of Life Science Companies and 34% Growth in the Number of Life Science Employees in Jerusalem Relative to 2006." Reuters.

Biojerusalem (2015). BioJeruselem. Retrieved from http://www.biojerusalem.org.il/

Boston Redevelopment Authority (2016). *Boston at a Glance - 2016.*

References

Botsman, R. (2015). "Defining The Sharing Economy: What Is Collaborative Consumption - and What Isn't?" Retrieved from https://www.fastcoexist.com/3046119/defining-the-sharing-economy-what-is-collaborative-consumption-and-what-isnt

Bradley, B. (2013). "Cleveland's Evergreen Cooperatives Finding Better Ways to Employ Locals, Keep Cash Flow in Town – Next City". Retrieved from https://nextcity.org/daily/entry/clevelands-evergreen-cooperatives-finding-better-ways-to-employ-locals-keep

BWK GmbH (2011). *Successful Start-ups in Berlin.*

CITIE (2015). "Regulation Disrupted: How Cities Are Responding." Retrieved from http://citie.org/stories/regulation-disrupted-how-cities-are-responding/

Cohen, M. (2015). *Urban Economic Challenges and the New Urban Agenda.* Nairobi: UN-Habitat, Urban Economy and Finance Branch.

Csomos, G. (2013). "The Command and Control Centers of the United States (2006/2012): An Analysis of Industry Sectors Influencing the Position of Cities." *Geoforum, 50* (pp. 241–251).

Daegu (2015). "Daegu to host IoT (Internet of Things) Healthcare Complex." Retrieved from http://english.daegu.go.kr/cms/cms.asp?Menu=521&BoardId=15219&Action=view

De Groene Zaak (2015). *Governments Going Circular.*

Deloitte (2014). *Value of Connectivity: Economic and Social Benefits of Expanding Internet Access.*

Demirgüç-Kunt, A. (2011). "Generating Jobs in Developing Countries: A Big Role for Small Firms - The World Bank Blog." Retrieved from http://blogs.worldbank.org/allaboutfinance/generating-jobs-in-developing-countries-a-big-role-for-small-firms

Dervojeda, K., Verzijl, D., Nagtegaal, F., Lengton, M., Rouwmaat, E., Monfardini, E., and Frideres, L. (2013). *The Sharing Economy: Accessibility Based Business Models for Peer-to-Peer Markets.* Directorate-General for Enterprise and Industry, European Commission.

Dobbs, R., Smit, S., Remes, J., Manyika, J., Roxburgh, C., and Restrepo, A. (2011). *Urban World : Mapping the Economic Power of Cities McKinsey Global Institute.* London: McKinsey Global Institute. Retrieved from http://www.mckinsey.com/insights/urbanization/urban_world

Dobbs, R., Remes, J., Manyika, J., Roxburgh, C., Smit, S., and Schaer, F. (2012). *Urban World: Cities and the Rise of the Consuming Class*. London: McKinsey Global Institute.

Dobbs, R., Remes, J., Smit, S., Manyika, J., Woetzel, J., and Agyenim-Boateng, Y. (2013). *Urban World: The Shifting Global Business Landscape*. London: McKinsey Global Institute.

Dobbs, R., Remes, J., Manyika, J., Woetzel, J., Perrey, J., Kelly, G., Pattabiraman, K., and Sharma, H. (2016). *Urban World: The Global Consumers To Watch*. McKinsey Global Institute.

Duranton, G. (2014). *Growing through Cities in Developing Countries*. Policy Research Working Papers; no. WPS 6818. Washington, D.C.: World Bank Group.

Enerbyte (2016). Enerbyte Virtual Energy Advisor. Retrieved from http://www.enerbyte.com/index.html

Euromonitor International (2016). Passport Database - Cities.

European Commission (2014). *Green Employment Initiative: Tapping into the job creation potential of the green economy. COM(2014) 446 final.*

European Commission (2015a). Communication from the Commission to the European Parliament, the Council, the European Economic and Social Committee and the Committee of the Regions. Closing the Loop - An EU action plan for the Circular Economy. *COM/2015/0614 final.*

European Commission (2015b). EURES-Labour market information. Retrieved from https://ec.europa.eu/eures/main.jsp?countryId=DE&acro=lmi&showRegion=true&lang=en&mode=text&regionId=DE0&nuts2Code=&nuts3Code=null&catId=375

European Commission (2016). Fact Sheet - A European Agenda for the Collaborative Economy. Retrieved from http://europa.eu/rapid/press-release_MEMO-16-2002_en.htm

European Environment Agency (2012). "Green Economy." Retrieved from http://www.eea.europa.eu/themes/economy/intro

European Union (2015). *Creating Value through Open Data: Study on the Impact of Re-use of Public Data Resources*. http://doi.org/10.2759/328101

Evergreen Cooperatives (2016). "Evergreen Cooperatives." Retrieved from http://www.evgoh.com/about-us/

References

EY (2015). *Cultural Times: The First Global Map of Cultural and Creative Industries*. Ernst & Young Global Limited.

Fayman, S., Keresztély, K., Meyer, P., Walsh, K., Pascual, J., Borja, F., Horelli, L., and Kukkonnen, H. (2011). *Good Policies and Practices to Tackle Urban Challenges*. Paris: ACT Consultants.

Fikri, K., and Zhu, T. J. (2015). *City Analytics : Competitive Cities for Jobs and Growth, Companion Paper 1*. Washington, D.C.: World Bank. https://openknowledge.worldbank.org/handle/10986/23569 License: CC BY 3.0 IGO.

Floater, G., Rode, P., Robert, A., Kennedy, C., Hoornweg, D., Slavcheva, R., and Godfrey, N. (2014). *Cities and the New Climate Economy: The Transformative Role of Global Urban Growth*. New Climate Economy Cities, Paper 01. LSE Cities, London School of Economics and Political Science, London, UK.

Furman, P. (2013). "Map this! New City Tech Tool Lets Small Businesses Compete with the Big Guys by Dishing Data." *NY Daily News*. Retrieved from http://www.nydailynews.com/new-york/map-new-city-tech-tool-lets-small-businesses-compete-big-guys-dishing-data-article-1.1559044

Gibson, J., Robinson, M., and Cain, S. (2015). *CITIE: City Initiatives for Technology, Innovation and Entrepreneurship*.

Glaeser (2015). "A New Urban Opportunity Agenda." *City Journal*.

Gonzales Rocha, E. A. (2012). "The Impact of the Business Environment on the Size of the Micro, Small and Medium Enterprise Sector; Preliminary Findings from a Cross-Country Comparison." *Procedia Economics and Finance*, 4 (pp. 335–349).

Hawksworth, J., and Vaughan, R. (2014). "The Sharing Economy – Sizing the Revenue Opportunity." Retrieved from http://www.pwc.co.uk/issues/megatrends/collisions/sharingeconomy/the-sharing-economy-sizing-the-revenue-opportunity.jhtml

Hermann, B. L., Gauthier, J., Holtschke, D., Bermann, R. D., and Marmer, M. (2015). *The Global Startup Ecosystem Ranking 2015*. The Startup Ecosystem Report Series. Startup Compass Inc.

Holtschke, D. (2016). "Berlin Startup Hub: The Rise to Europe's Startup Capital." Retrieved from http://startupgeist.com/berlin-startup-hub/

Howkins, J. (n.d.) "The Creative Economy." Retrieved from http://www.johnhowkins.com/wordpress/

References

IHK, and HWK (2015). *Berlin's Economy in Figures - 2015 Issue*. Berlin: Industrie und Handelskammer Berlin and Handwerkskammer Berlin (HWK).

ILO (2016a). "Informal Economy." Retrieved October 5, 2016, from http://www.ilo.org/global/topics/employment-promotion/informal-economy/lang--en/index.htm

ILO (2016b). *World Employment Social Outlook: Trends 2016*. Geneva: International Labour Organization (ILO).

Innovation District (2015). Boston's Innovation District. Retrieved from http://www.innovationdistrict.org/

Katz, B. J., and Wagner, J. (2014). "The Rise of Urban Innovation Districts." *Harvard Business Review*.

Kilroy, A., Francis, L., Mukim, M., and Negri, S. (2015). *Competitive Cities for Jobs and Growth: What, Who and How*. Washington, D.C.: World Bank Group. Retrieved from http://documents.worldbank.org/curated/en/2015/12/25515215/competitive-cities-jobs-growth

Koopman, C., Mitchell, M., and Thierer, A. (2014). *The Sharing Economy and Consumer Protection Regulation: The Case for Policy Change*. Arlington, VA: Mercatus Center at George Mason University.

Kulenovic, Z. J., and Cech, A. (2015). *Six Case Studies of Economically Successful Cities*. Washington, D.C.: World Bank Group.

Lall, S. V (2016). *Getting Cities to Work*. (The East and Central African Cities Development Forum & 2016. Kampala, May 24-26, Eds.). The World Bank Group.

Manyika, J., Chui, M., Groves, P., Farrell, D., Van Kuiken, S., and Doshi, E. A. (2013). *Open Data: Unlocking Innovation and Performance with Liquid Information*. McKinsey Global Institute.

McKinsey Berlin (2013). *Berlin Builds Businesses: Five Initiatives for Europe's Start-up Hub*. Berlin: McKinsey & Company, Inc.

McLaren, D., and Agyeman, J. (2016). "Sharing Strikes Back: A New Era of Urban Commoning." *The World Financial Review. Empowering Communication Globally*. Retrieved from http://www.worldfinancialreview.com/?p=8961

McLaren, D., and Agyeman, J. (2015). *Sharing Cities: A Case for Truly Smart and Sustainable Cities*. MIT Press, Cambridge, MA.

New Climate Economy (2014). *Better Growth, Better Climate: The New Climate Economy Report*. Washington D.C.: The Global Commission on the Economy and Climate. Retrieved from http://newclimateeconomy.report/

References

NLC (2013). "Cleveland Green Jobs Using a Cooperative." Retrieved from http://www.nlc.org/find-city-solutions/city-solutions-and-applied-research/city-practice-database/cleveland-ohio-green-jobs-using-a-cooperative

NYC Global Partners (2010). *Best Practice: Initiative to Foster Economic Growth in the BioMedical Sector.*

OECD (2015). *The Metropolitan Century: Understanding Urbanisation and its Consequences Policy Highlights*. Paris: OECD Publishing.

Open Data Handbook (2012). "What is Open Data?" Retrieved from http://opendatahandbook.org/guide/en/what-is-open-data/

Oxford Economics (2014). *Future Trends and Market Opportunities in the World's Largest 750 Cities: How the Global Urban Landscape Will Look in 2030 - Executive Summary.* Retrieved from https://www.oxfordeconomics.com/Media/Default/landing-pages/cities/OE-cities-summary.pdf

Palacios, J. (2005). "Economic Agglomeration and Industrial Clustering in Developing Countries: The Case of the Mexican Silicon Valley." In A. Kuchiki, J. Sun & J. Palacios (eds.), *Joint Research Program Series*, No. 137, 161-271.

Porter, M. E. (1995). "The Competitive Advantage of the Inner City," *Harvard Business Review, 73*(3), (pp. 55-71).

Porter, M. E. (1998). "On Competition," *Harvard Business Review, 98609*, (pp. 77–90).

Porter, M. E. (2000). "Location, Competition, and Economic Development: Local Clusters in a Global Economy," *Economic Development Quarterly, 14* (1), (pp. 15–34).

Ramirez, E., and Youn-joo, S. (2012). "Youth Start-up Programs Young, but Blooming," *The Korea Herald*. Retrieved from http://www.koreaherald.com/common_prog/newsprint.php?ud=20121002000722&dt=2

Rodriguez, H., Congdon, D., and Ampelas, V. (2015). *The Development of Boston's Innovation District: A Case Study of Cross-Sector Collaboration and Public Entrepreneurship.* New York: The Intersector Project, Inc.

Sassen, S. (2008). "Cities in Today's Global Age: An Exploration of the New Economic Role of Cities and the Networks They Form in an Increasingly Globalised World." In *Connecting Cities: Networks (A Research Publication of the 9th World Congress of Metropolis).* Metropolis Congress.

Seoul Solution (2014). "Youth's Business 1000." Retrieved from https://seoulsolution.kr/content/youth%E2%80%99s-business-1000?language=en

Share Hub (2015). *Seoul Sharing City Executive Summary in 2015.*

The Economist (2014). *Transforming Cities - Special Edition.* Retrieved from https://www.rockefellerfoundation.org/app/uploads/Transforming-Cities.pdf

Toly, N., and Tabory, S. (2016). *100 Top Economies: Urban Influence and the Position of Cities in an Evolving World Order.* The Chicago Council on Global Affairs.

UNEP (2013). *City-Level Decoupling: Urban Resource Flows and the Governance of Infrastructure Transitions. A Report of the Working Group on Cities of the International Resource Panel.* Swilling M., Robinson B., Marvin S. and Hodson M.

UNESCO (n.d.). "Creative Industries." Retrieved from http://www.unesco.org/new/en/santiago/culture/creative-industries/

UN-Habitat (2016). *Urbanization and Development: Emerging Futures. World Cities Report 2016.* Nairobi: United Nations Human Settlements Programme (UN-HABITAT).

United Nations (2014). *Some Facts on Urbanisation.* ECOSOC - Integration Segment (May 27-29, 2014). Retrieved from http://www.un.org/en/ecosoc/integration/pdf/fact_sheet.pdf

Verhulst, S., and Young, A. (2016). *The Global Impact of Open Data: Key Findings from Detailed Case Studies Around the World.*

Watson, J., and Freudmann, A. (2011). *Fostering Innovation-led Clusters: A Review of Leading Global Practices.* London: The Economist Intelligence Unit Ltd.

Webber, J. (2015). "Guadalajara: Mexico's Second City is a Latin "Silicon Valley"." *Financial Times.* Retrieved from http://www.ft.com/cms/s/0/ec7461a8-ffb3-11e4-bc30-00144feabdc0.html#axzz3mMmdljBv

WEF (2014). *The Competitiveness of Cities.* Geneva: World Economic Forum (WEF).

WEF (2016). *Inspiring Future Cities & Urban Services Shaping the Future of Urban Development & Services Initiative.* Geneva: World Economic Forum (WEF). Retrieved from http://www3.weforum.org/docs/WEF_Urban-Services.pdf

Weiss, M. A. (2006). *Cities and Urban Regions as Engines of Economic Growth.* USAID Training.

Wilcox, M., and Voskoglou, C. (2015). *European App Economy Report 2015.* London: Vision Mobile.

WISP (2016). Western Cape Industrial Symbiosis Programme. Retrieved from http://greencape.co.za/wisp/

References

World Bank (2000). "Dynamic Cities as Engines of Growth." *World Development Report 1999/2000* (pp. 125–138).

Young, A., Sangokoya, D., and Verhulst, S. (2016). "Open Data's Impact: The New York City Business Atlas-Leveling the Playing Field." Retrieved from www.odimpact.org

Zeng, D. Z. (2010). *Building Engines for Growth and Competitiveness in China*. Washington, D.C.: World Bank Group.

Zeng, D. Z. (2015). "Global Experiences with Special Economic Zones: Focus on China and Africa." *World Bank Policy Research Paper*, (WPS7240), (pp. 1–17).

6. Appendix I: Additional Resources

On the IESE Cities in Motion Strategies website you will find additional related material and resources. Check the following links regularly to access our latest publications:

- IESE Cities in Motion Strategies: http://www.iese.edu/cim.

Additionally, the authors recommend the following internet resources for more information on the topic:

- 100 resilient cities: http://www.100resilientcities.org.
- C40 Cities: http://www.c40.org.
- Cities Alliance: http://www.citiesalliance.org.
- CITYLAB: http://www.citylab.com.
- CIVITAS Initiative: http://www.civitas.eu.
- Collaborative Consumption: http://www.collaborativeconsumption.com.
- Creative Cities Network: http://en.unesco.org/creative-cities.
- Ellen MacArthur Foundation (Circular Economy): https://www.ellenmacarthurfoundation.org.
- EUROCITIES: http://www.eurocities.eu.
- European Network of Living Labs: http://www.openlivinglabs.eu.
- Global Cities Business Alliance: https://www.businessincities.com.
- Global Cities Initiative – The Brookings Institution: http://www.brookings.edu/about/projects/global-cities
- Grow Smarter: http://www.grow-smarter.eu.
- Leading Cities: http://leadingcities.org.

Appendix I: Additional Resources

- Metropolis - http://www.metropolis.org.
- National League of Cities - http://www.nlc.org.
- ICLEI – Local Governments for Sustainability: http://www.iclei.org.
- New Cities Foundation - http://www.newcitiesfoundation.org.
- OECD – Urban Development - http://www.oecd.org/regional/regional-policy/urbandevelopment.htm.
- Open Data Handbook - http://opendatahandbook.org.
- Smart Cities Council - http://smartcitiescouncil.com.
- Sustainable Cities Platform - http://www.sustainablecities.eu.
- The Circulars - https://thecirculars.org.
- UN-Habitat - http://unhabitat.org.
- UN-Population Fund - http://www.unfpa.org/urbanization.
- UN-World Urbanization Prospects: http://esa.un.org/unpd/wup.
- URBACT: http://urbact.eu.
- World Bank - http://www.worldbank.org.
- World Resources Institute (WRI): http://www.wri.org.

7. Appendix II: Cities in Motion Index – Economic Dimension

This appendix includes a brief presentation of the IESE Cities in Motion Index, focusing on the economic dimension. For more information on the index, please check the IESE Cities in Motion website www.iese.edu/cim, with all our latest publications.

CITIES IN MOTION INDEX

The Cities in Motion Index (*CIMI*) has been designed with the aim of constructing a "breakthrough" indicator in terms of its completeness, characteristics, comparability and the quality and objectivity of its information. Its goal is to enable measurement of the future sustainability of the world's main cities, as well as the quality of life of their inhabitants.

The *CIMI* aims to help the public and governments understand the performance of 10 fundamental dimensions for a city: governance, urban planning, public management, technology, the environment, international outreach, social cohesion, mobility and transportation, human capital, and the economy. Thanks to its broad and integrated vision of the city, the Cities in Motion Index provides insights on the strengths and weaknesses of each city, allowing the identification of effective solutions.

The 2016 edition is the third consecutive *CIMI*, covering the years 2013, 2014 and 2015. It includes a total of 181 cities, of which 72 are capitals

Appendix II: Cities in Motion Index – Economic Dimension

representing more than 80 different countries, as well as 77 indicators measuring the 10 relevant dimensions.

RANKING *CIMI* 2015

New York City (United States) is in the first place in the overall ranking, driven by its performance in the dimensions of the economy (first place), technology (third place) and in human capital, public management, governance, international outreach, and mobility and transportation (fourth place). However, for another year, it has ranked very low in the dimensions of social cohesion (position 161) and the environment (position 93). After New York, London (UK) is ranked in second place and Paris (France) in third.

Of the 10 top positions of the ranking, four cities are in the U.S. (New York, San Francisco, Boston and Chicago); four cities are in Europe (London, Paris, Amsterdam and Geneva); one is in Asia (Seoul) and one in Oceania (Sydney).

TABLE A1. CITY RANKING. TOP 10

CIMI 2015	City (Country)
1	New York City (United States)
2	London (United Kingdom)
3	Paris (France)
4	San Francisco (United States)
5	Boston (United States)
6	Amsterdam (Netherlands)
7	Chicago (United States)
8	Seoul (South Korea)
9	Geneva (Switzerland)
10	Sydney (Australia)

Appendix II: Cities in Motion Index – Economic Dimension

DIMENSION: THE ECONOMY

This dimension includes all those aspects that promote the economic development of a territory: local economic development plans, transition plans, strategic industrial plans, and cluster generation, innovation and entrepreneurial initiatives.

The indicators used to represent the performance of cities in the economic dimension are specified in Table A2, along with descriptions of them, their units of measurement and the sources of information.

TABLE A2. ECONOMIC INDICATORS

Indicator	Description / Unit of measurement	Source
Productivity	Labor productivity calculated as GDP/working population (in thousands)	Euromonitor
Time required to start a business	Number of calendar days needed so a business can operate legally	World Bank
Ease of starting a business	Ease of starting a business. Top positions in the ranking indicate a more favorable regulatory environment for creating and operating a local company	World Bank
Number of headquarters	Number of headquarters of publicly traded companies	Globalization and World Cities (GaWC)
Percentage of people at early business stage	Percentage of 18 to 64-year-old population who are new entrepreneurs or owners/managers of a new business	Global Entrepreneurship Monitor
Entrepreneurs	Companies in an initial phase that represent a city's economic bases. They represent economic dynamism and include a high proportion of companies devoted to technology. Used per capita	2thinknow
GDP	Gross domestic product in millions of U.S. dollars at 2014 prices	Euromonitor

Appendix II: Cities in Motion Index – Economic Dimension

Considering that the **CIMI** seeks to measure, via multiple dimensions, sustainability into the future of the world's main cities and the quality of life of their inhabitants, real GDP is a measure of the city's economic power and of its inhabitants' income. In addition, it is an important measure of the quality of life in cities. In numerous studies, GDP is considered the only or the most important measure of the performance of a city or country. However, in this report, it is not considered as exclusive nor as the most important measure: it is considered as one more indicator within one of the 10 dimensions of the **CIMI**. Thus, its share of the total is similar to that of other indicators. For example, a city with a high or relatively high GDP, if it does not have a good performance in other indicators, may not be in one of the top positions. In this way, a city that is very productive but has problems with transportation, inequality, weak public finance or a production process that uses polluting technology probably will not be in the top positions of the ranking.

Labor productivity is a measure of the strength, efficiency and technological level of the production system, which, with regard to local and international competitiveness, will have repercussions, obviously, on real salaries, on capital income, on business profits. For this reason, it is very important to consider the measure in the economic dimension, since different productivity rates can explain differences in the quality of life of a city's workers – and on the sustainability over time of the production system.

The other indicators selected as representative of this dimension enable the measurement of several aspects of a city's business landscape, such as the number of headquarters of publicly traded companies; the entrepreneurial capacity and possibilities of a city's inhabitants, represented by the percentage of people at an early business stage; entrepreneurial companies; the time required to start a business; and the ease of starting a business in regulatory terms. These indicators measure a city's sustainability capacity over time and the potential ability to improve the quality of life of its inhabitants. The time required to start a business and the ease of launching it are incorporated into the economic dimension with a negative sign, since lower values indicate a greater ease of starting businesses. The number of headquarters of publicly traded companies, the capacity, the number of entrepreneurs and the entrepreneurial possibilities of a city's inhabitants have a positive relationship, since the high values of these indicators reflect the economic dynamism of a city and the ease of allowing the installation and development of new businesses.

RANKING – ECONOMIC DIMENSION

The city that heads the ranking in this dimension is New York City (United States). This city achieves relatively high levels in all indicators but it stands out especially for its high GDP and number of headquarters of publicly traded companies. It is important to mention that the top 10 for this dimension has eight U.S. cities.

TABLE A3. RANKING BY DIMENSION: THE ECONOMY

City, Country	Economic Ranking	CIMI 2015 Ranking
New York City, United States	1	1
San Francisco, United States	2	4
London, United Kingdom	3	2
Los Angeles, United States	4	15
Tokyo, Japan	5	12
Houston, United States	6	31
Chicago, United States	7	7
Boston, United States	8	5
Washington, D.C., United States	9	13
Dallas, United States	10	19
Paris, France	11	3

Appendix II: Cities in Motion Index – Economic Dimension

City, Country	Economic Ranking	CIMI 2015 Ranking
Philadelphia, United States	12	23
Baltimore, United States	13	18
Geneva, Switzerland	14	9
Abu Dhabi, United Arab Emirates	15	66
Miami, United States	16	53
Toronto, Canada	17	24
Sydney, Australia	18	10
Zurich, Switzerland	19	14
Seoul, South Korea	20	8
Phoenix, United States	21	40
Hong Kong, China	22	39
Dublin, Ireland	23	36
London, Canada	24	37
Singapore, Singapore	25	22
Melbourne, Australia	26	17
Amsterdam, Netherlands	27	6
Oslo, Norway	28	28
Haifa, Israel	29	101
Doha, Qatar	30	117
Vancouver, Canada	31	20
Stockholm, Sweden	32	27
Montreal, Canada	33	38
Copenhagen, Denmark	34	11
Gothenburg, Sweden	35	57
Basel, Switzerland	36	42
Santiago, Chile	37	80
Nottingham, United Kingdom	38	75
Liverpool, United Kingdom	39	48
Osaka, Japan	40	56

Appendix II: Cities in Motion Index — Economic Dimension

City, Country	Economic Ranking	CIMI 2015 Ranking
Munich, Germany	41	21
Stuttgart, Germany	42	51
Birmingham, United Kingdom	43	47
Brussels, Belgium	44	32
Helsinki, Finland	45	25
Manchester, United Kingdom	46	43
Glasgow, United Kingdom	47	46
Frankfurt, Germany	48	35
Tel Aviv, Israel	49	97
Eindhoven, Netherlands	50	59
Auckland, New Zealand	51	29
Ottawa, Canada	52	30
Vienna, Austria	53	26
Leeds, United Kingdom	54	71
Rotterdam, Netherlands	55	70
Mexico City, Mexico	56	100
Bangkok, Thailand	57	84
Lima, Peru	58	122
Hamburg, Germany	59	41
Lyon, France	60	55
Milan, Italy	61	44
Guadalajara, Mexico	62	116
Cologne, Germany	63	52
Monterrey, Mexico	64	102
Berlin, Germany	65	16
Medellin, Colombia	66	99
Nice, France	67	61
Lille, France	68	79
Antwerp, Belgium	69	77

Appendix II: Cities in Motion Index – Economic Dimension

City, Country	Economic Ranking	CIMI 2015 Ranking
Madrid, Spain	70	34
Tallinn, Estonia	71	54
Lisbon, Portugal	72	62
Marseille, France	73	72
Bilbao, Spain	74	69
Riyadh, Saudi Arabia	75	123
Bratislava, Slovakia	76	83
Rome, Italy	77	81
Nagoya, Japan	78	87
Barcelona, Spain	79	33
Vilnius, Lithuania	80	89
Beijing, China	81	92
Cali, Colombia	82	126
Duisburg, Germany	83	73
Riga, Latvia	84	78
Porto, Portugal	85	76
Jerusalem, Israel	86	105
Florence, Italy	87	50
Bogota, Colombia	88	111
Turin, Italy	89	82
Istanbul, Turkey	90	109
Busan, South Korea	91	91
Daejeon, South Korea	92	96
Daegu, South Korea	93	98
Manama, Bahrein	94	138
Valencia, Spain	95	49
Shanghai, China	96	93
Sofia, Bulgaria	97	95
Linz, Austria	98	63

Appendix II: Cities in Motion Index – Economic Dimension

City, Country	Economic Ranking	CIMI 2015 Ranking
Seville, Spain	99	67
A Coruna, Spain	100	60
Lagos, Nigeria	101	180
Dubai, United Arab Emirates	102	65
Taipei, Taiwan	103	64
Kuala Lumpur, Malaysia	104	88
Bursa, Turkey	105	128
Athens, Greece	106	113
Kaohsiung, Taiwan	107	103
Taichung, Taiwan	108	112
Ljubljana, Slovenia	109	86
Guangzhou, China	110	104
Bucharest, Romania	111	110
Shenzhen, China	112	130
Warsaw, Poland	113	74
Naples, Italy	114	90
Douala, Cameroon	115	175
Moscow, Russia	116	108
Ankara, Turkey	117	127
Baku, Azerbaijan	118	150
Tianjin, China	119	166
Montevideo, Uruguay	120	121
Wroclaw, Poland	121	94
Budapest, Hungary	122	68
Malaga, Spain	123	58
Tbilisi, Georgia	124	135
Quito, Ecuador	125	132
Prague, Czech Republic	126	45
Guatemala City, Guatemala	127	161

Appendix II: Cities in Motion Index – Economic Dimension

City, Country	Economic Ranking	CIMI 2015 Ranking
Guayaquil, Ecuador	128	148
Minsk, Belarus	129	137
Jidda, Saudi Arabia	130	115
Almaty, Kazakhstan	131	125
Wuhan, China	132	153
Tainan, Taiwan	133	141
Skopje, Macedonia	134	146
Belgrade, Serbia	135	114
Casablanca, Morocco	136	163
Manila, Philippines	137	145
Johannesburg, South Africa	138	140
Zagreb, Croatia	139	107
Pretoria, South Africa	140	164
Buenos Aires, Argentina	141	85
Durban, South Africa	142	159
Kuwait, Kuwait	143	119
Santo Domingo, Dominican Republic	144	172
Cape Town, South Africa	145	120
Sao Paulo, Brazil	146	124
Suzhou, China	147	165
Shenyang, China	148	155
Harbin, China	149	169
Cordoba, Argentina	150	106
San Jose, Costa Rica	151	131
Rosario, Argentina	152	134
Chongqing, China	153	147
Tehran, Iran	154	177
Ho Chi Minh City, Vietnam	155	158
Amman, Jordan	156	160

Appendix II: Cities in Motion Index – Economic Dimension

City, Country	Economic Ranking	CIMI 2015 Ranking
La Paz, Bolivia	157	168
Kiev, Ukraine	158	143
Saint Petersburg, Russia	159	133
Tunis, Tunisia	160	144
Jakarta, Indonesia	161	170
Novosibirsk, Russia	162	154
Santa Cruz, Bolivia	163	171
Cairo, Egypt	164	156
Porto Alegre, Brazil	165	118
Curitiba, Brazil	166	129
Brasilia, Brazil	167	136
Nairobi, Kenya	168	178
Rio de Janeiro, Brazil	169	139
Karachi, Pakistan	170	181
Alexandria, Egypt	171	173
Sarajevo, Bosnia and Herzegovina	172	157
Belo Horizonte, Brazil	173	152
Recife, Brazil	174	142
Fortaleza, Brazil	175	149
Bombay, India	176	167
Salvador, Brazil	177	151
Delhi, India	178	174
Bangalore, India	179	176
Kolkata, India	180	179
Caracas, Venezuela	181	162

www.ingramcontent.com/pod-product-compliance
Lightning Source LLC
Chambersburg PA
CBHW060348190526
45169CB00002B/528